TROUBLED SPIRITS
with
LORAINE REES:

A Medium's Conversations
with Jack the Ripper and other Spirits

by

Mary Ross, PhD

Oxshott Press

TROUBLED SPIRITS WITH LORAINE REES: A MEDIUM'S CONVERSATIONS WITH JACK THE RIPPER AND OTHER SPIRITS

READER' FAVORITE
* * * * * FIVE STARS OUT OF FIVE * * * * *

"Fascinating, especially the Ripper walk... An impressive and well-written book that gave me a lot to think about. I'm glad I read it and recommend it to others with an interest in parapsychology and spiritualism.

-- Jack Magnus, READER'S FAVORITE

"Found it fascinating and quite different to other books I've read on the subject. Loraine is indeed seriously gifted, and... those sketches were really sensitive."

-- Sally Spedding, Multi-awarded Crime Mystery Writer

TROUBLED SPIRITS

with

LORAINE REES:

A Medium's Conversations with Jack the Ripper and other Spirits

by

Mary Ross, PhD

Published by: Oxshott Press
Edited by: Margaret Saine
Cover design: Jane Ubell-Meyer

SECOND EDITION
Copyright ©2024 by Mary Ross

Original Copyright ©2013 by Mary Ross

ISBN 9781736023495

Photos by M. Ross
and from the private collection of Loraine Rees
unless otherwise noted.

Contact:

Loraine Rees School of Psychic Studies on Facebook

Or

OXSHOTT PRESS
P.O. Box 718
Neshanic Station, NJ 08853

For my family

ALSO BY DR. MARY ROSS

Meet Loraine Rees and follow four years of her practice in this insightful portrayal of a modern medium at work. Published in 2011, Dr. Ross' first book on medium Loraine Rees includes Loraine's personal history, from how Loraine came to understand her remarkable abilities to her near-death experiences as the medium shares what she learned on the other side.

"There is much reassurance, comfort, and humor in Ross' book as spirits eager to confirm their continued presence in a loved one's life expose family secrets in public readings... Dr. Ross' book conveys the good news that each human being is much more than can be seen with the eyes."

-- Kristine Morris, Foreword Clarion Reviews

And

An Amazon Best-Seller

Join Medium Loraine Rees and Award-winning Author Mary
Ross, PhD, as she documents the wisdom Loraine channels from
beyond. Learn how to manifest your destiny and join a new phase
in human evolution.

The author (left) with Loraine

ACKNOWLEDGEMENTS

We would like to say a big thank you to everyone who participated in the events in this book and those who contributed to its production. Special thanks to Kathy, Dr. Hisham Daghestani, and the film crew on the Jack the Ripper ghost walk.

We would also like to thank those who continue to be a guiding presence in our lives.

  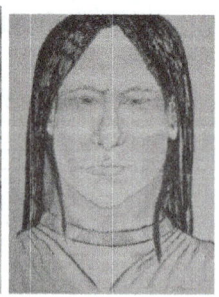

MAP OF LOCATIONS

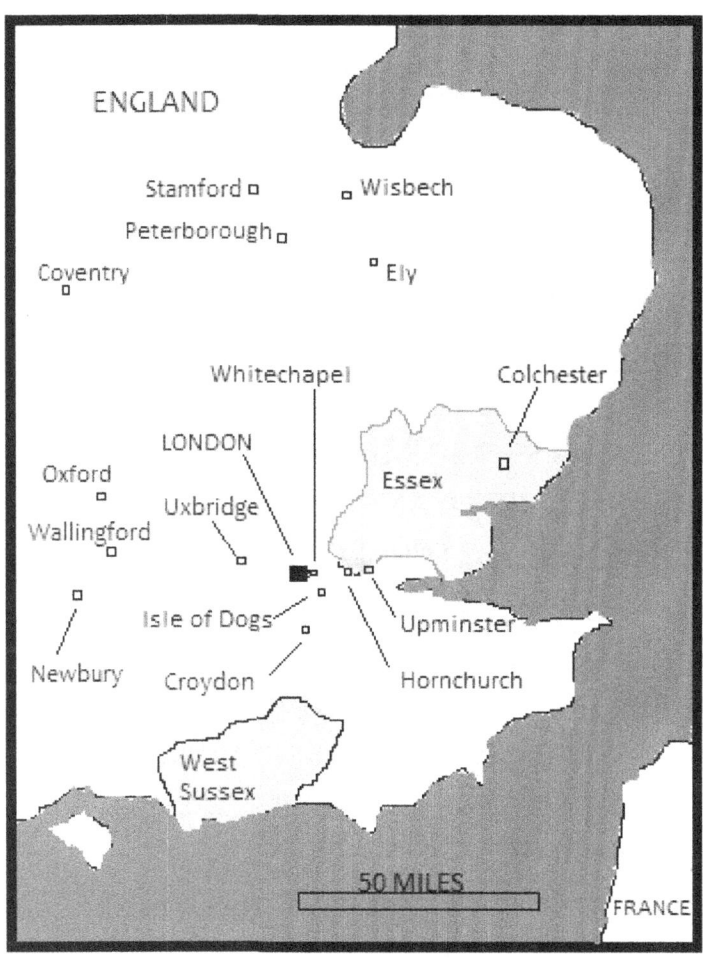

TABLE OF CONTENTS

ALSO BY DR. MARY ROSS 6

ACKNOWLEDGEMENTS 8

MAP OF LOCATIONS 9

LIST OF FIGURES 11

INTRODUCTION 13

CHAPTER 1. THE ELY GHOST WALK 19

CHAPTER 2. THE WISBECH GHOST WALK 30

CHAPTER 3. A PSYCHIC SKETCH ARTIST 35

CHAPTER 4. CLAIRVOYANT EVENING 45

CHAPTER 5. THE HORNCHURCH SHOW 63

CHAPTER 6. DEBUNKING DISBELIEF 82

CHAPTER 7. NEWBURY 90

CHAPTER 8. JACK THE RIPPER GHOST WALK 97

CHAPTER 9. JACK THE RIPPER SECOND READING 115

CHAPTER 10. AN ANGRY MOTHER 145

ONE FINAL PHOTO 185

APPENDIX A – AN INTERVIEW WITH LORAINE 186

APPENDIX B: WHAT PEOPLE SAY 194

APPENDIX C: BOOKS BY DR. GARY SCHWARTZ 196

GLOSSARY OF PARAPSYCHOLOGY TERMS 198

ABOUT THE AUTHOR 204

LIST OF FIGURES

Loraine Rees	3
The Author with Loraine; Friends	8
Map of Locations	9
Loraine	19
Neil Humphries, Ghost Detective	21
Loraine "Heard" from Two Young Men who Drowned	23
Photo of Glowing Image on Cathedral Green, Ely	27
Neil Humphries	31
Mathew Hopkins, Witchfinder General	34
Sketch of Ramos	37
Charme and her Teddy-boy Dad	41
Alison and her Gran	42
Jane and her Father-in-law	43
Loraine with Mandy, Wallingford Fundraiser	45
Chris and his aunt	48
Pam, Jess, and Mum	49
Pam and Jess Examine the Sketch	50
Jan and her Mother-in-law	52
Pat with a Male Sprit	57
Pat's Bother Art	58
Diane and her sister, Carol	66
Joanne and her sister, Shelly	70
Julie and her daughter, Natasha	72
Loraine at the Hornchurch Show	75
Mandy and her father	77

Ancient Map Showing Purgatory   84

Ancient Flat-Earth map   89

Debbie's Daughter with her Family   92

Debbie's Grandmother, Lillian   93

Loraine, Neil, and Ripperologist Lawrence Summers   98

Sketching at Dunward Street   99

Sketch at Sight of Ripper Murder   99

Historic Sketch of Mary Anne Nichols   100

Sketch Where Martha Tabrum was Found   103

Historic Sketch of Martha Tabrum's Discovery   103

Loraine Demonstrates What the Ripper Did   105

Crest   105

Listening to Loraine at Mitre Square   108

Loraine Surrounded by Orbs   113

Historic Sketches of the Ripper Case   114

Dr. Thomas Cream   135

Robert D'Onston   138

Newgate Prison Gallows   140

First Sketch of Kathy's Mother   148

Second Sketch of Kathy's Mother   151

Kathy Wanted a Special Sign   181

One Final Photograph   185

Loraine Being Interviewed   186

Loraine at the Interview   193

The Author   204

INTRODUCTION

We all have different talents. Most talents can be refined with practice but not all can be. Some of us are blessed with rare natural gifts and abilities that few others can aspire to achieve. One such person is Loraine Rees, a clairvoyant medium who routinely speaks with, and sees, the dead. That probably sounds strange to you, but for Loraine, it's as normal and as easy as talking on the phone. She has had this ability her entire life, passed along to her by heredity through a long line of gifted psychics and clairvoyants. How she discovered her gift at an early age and the way she incorporates it into her work is chronicled in our first collaboration, <u>Love and Laughter with Spirit: Meet the Medium Loraine Rees</u>, published in 2011.

For me, that first book was a real journey of discovery as I initially met Loraine in 2007, then came to understand her talent more and more as I followed her around England over the next four years. Documenting her work for the book provided such extraordinary experiences that I didn't think there was anything more I could possibly write about her. But shortly after that first book was released, I was surprised when she told me it was just the start of our collaborations. According to Loraine, she has been "advised" that I will complete several more books on her and eventually write an entire series.

I was sceptical at first, unsure what more I could possibly say or write about her given the range of outrageous events and situations I had already seen as part of her practice. But within a year, Loraine expanded her horizons to include a series of ghost walks with detective Neil Humphries. One of those ghost walks, held in the Whitechapel District in London, searched for clues on the most notorious serial killer of all time, Jack the Ripper. As usual when Loraine goes to work, the results are nothing short of incredible.

After the publication of that first book, to my great surprise, I learned some things about myself and my own connection with the psychic world that could, at times, assist Loraine in her work. No doubt it was my association with Loraine that encouraged my own psychic talent as a psychic sketch artist to manifest on occasion. This ability, while useful when it works, pales in comparison to Loraine's steady and reliable ability to communicate with the other side. Still, I realized that when I do get a drawing right, it can be a meaningful accessory to Loraine's important work in bringing confirmation from beyond. I also realized that there was much more to learn and convey about Loraine and her work after all, and the nucleus of this second book took shape.

One of the most important revelations Loraine has received from the spirit world, as discussed in the first book, is that there IS a God being. Apparently, the spirits of departed souls can recognize this being when they are in the presence of it. This made me wonder. Why is it that spirits can recognize when they are in the presence of the God being? Is there some tiny spark of goodness that each of us carries inside us? Is this what makes us enjoy a book or a film with a happy ending? And what makes us cheer when the Chilean miners come out of the mine shaft, even if we've never been to Chile or climbed down a mine shaft? Does each of us carry a tiny spark of "rightness" inside us that makes us feel happy when it is kindled -- a basic thirst for "goodness"?

I have to wonder if our time on this physical world is a testing ground to prove the strength of our ability to embrace our inner goodness. It seems to me that all too often, we allow our physical needs and desires to overshadow what we feel or know to be right: the need for land can turn into wars; the need for food and shelter can turn into greed. Deviating from our own spark of goodness can cause us to injure or damage another being or infringe on someone else's rights in our quest for getting our own way.

None of us has a perfect record and we are all tempted from time to time to engage in actions that we wouldn't appreciate from others. But I have come to believe that if a person tries his best, accepts when he has deviated from what his conscience tells him is right, and does what he can to make amends, that he can find peace in the afterlife.

If that is true, what happens if a person has committed terrible acts against his fellow man and fails to accept responsibility for those actions? If a person refuses to feel remorse for the damages he has inflicted, what happens to his soul? What happens to the spirits who can not find peace?

According to what Loraine has gleaned from her links with beyond, when these damaged souls enter the spirit world, some can be redeemed, although not all can. Still others are too ashamed to enter the higher plane of the spirit world, afraid of what awaits them. Although they no longer have a physical form, their souls linger, trapped to remain on the physical plane, but without a physical form.

Loraine's encounters with such spirits are discussed in this book. Some of them have displayed great anger and negative energy that can be felt long after their deaths. In some cases, the impact of their energy has manifested in the physical world and the effects can be observed, including several instances discussed within these pages.

Some of these tormented souls are the residual energies of unrepentant murderers. Still others are their victims, whose energies have returned, perhaps to try to understand and come to terms with what happened to them.

The events required for a soul to be so deeply troubled are by nature quite extreme. I give you fair warning that some of the material reported in this book is tragic and violent. Consider yourself warned.

Yet if we can learn from the mistakes of others, I feel there is value in exploring and understanding the extreme cases of these troubled souls. And in Chapter 10, a story of horrible abuse, there is strong evidence that the soul can continue to evolve after death and that even a ravaged and tormented spirit might eventually be able to find peace.

Having watched Loraine channel some deeply troubled souls throughout the course of researching this book, I find it comforting that that even after death, a broken soul might be able to evolve into something better. With this in mind, I bring you these tales of troubled or restless spirits, much of it told from beyond the grave.

It is Loraine's special gift as a "psychic telephone" that makes this possible.

Despite the dark subject matter contained in various sections within this volume, the underlying message of this book is that there is hope for us all if we choose to embrace our inner goodness. I am pleased to document these true stories in this second book on Loraine Rees and her work.

Read on and listen in when that very special telephone starts to ring.

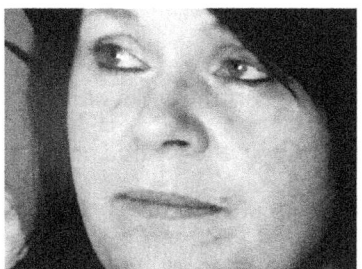

CHAPTER 1. THE ELY GHOST WALK
KINGS, QUEENS, and CLERICS
SEPT. 2011

Neil Humphries, a police detective formerly with Scotland Yard, met Loraine in 2009 when a fellow officer had asked him to help on an insurance case that Loraine was filing. The officer told Neil about Loraine's abilities as they were well known to the various police authorities in helping solve difficult cases.

One example of this was a case a few years previously in the Cambridge area where two girls had gone missing. The police questioned the friends and family but could find no leads. They were so stumped that they invited Loraine and some other psychics to see if they could help. It was Loraine who told the investigative team that there was a school connection, and that the girls had been taken by a man who worked at their school. Out of respect for the families, Loraine will not publicly reveal the specifics of the case. Suffice it to say that when the police investigated what she told them, they found the man and he was promptly arrested.

When Neil met Loraine, he had been a detective a long time and had seen a lot of things. Having joined the Metropolitan Police in 1976, he served in both uniform and detective roles until 2008 when he became a criminal justice and investigations expert who runs his own consultancy and promotions businesses. Trained to be sceptical, at first he wasn't sure what to believe. As a detective, he always looks for a logical explanation. But where Loraine was concerned, there didn't seem to be any rational explanation for her information when she gave him a message from a friend of his who had recently died. Loraine provided the friend's first name, the way he had died, and explained how it had happened. These were details that had not been reported in the newspaper or anywhere else. She provided additional information as well that was too specific to deny and wouldn't be possible for her to have -- *unless she actually did speak with the dead.*

Neil and Loraine first discussed the idea of hosting ghost walks in the summer of 2011. Neil knew that Loraine could pick up information on a one-to-one basis and at her various indoor shows but he wasn't sure what would happen in a casual outdoors

NEIL HUMPHRIES, the ghost detective,
formerly with Scotland Yard

setting. On 31 August 2011, they held a trial ghost walk on the River Thames. As soon as they started to walk along the river, Loraine began picking up a number of energies and even a cursory examination showed Neil she was onto something.

Neil was sold. They decided to host a second ghost walk and invite people to come along with Neil acting as Loraine's official "ghost detective." For the setting of this second ghost walk, Neil chose the town of Ely, a place with a long and chequered history. Located southeast of Peterborough, Ely has been the site of a religious base since 695 AD when the Saxon Queen Etheldreda founded a religious order and built a monastery.

In the years that followed, the town had a strong association with various bishops who, during medieval times, were nearly as powerful as the royalty. Ely also boasts connections with King

Charles I, Henry VIII, and Oliver Cromwell. As a detective and a lover of mysteries, Neil felt that Ely's rich and royal history, full of political intrigue and ripe with dark tales of wrong-doing, would be the perfect setting for an outdoor evening of clairvoyance with Loraine.

The "Kings, Queens, and Clerics" event was held in Ely on 26 September 2011. The group consisted of about 20 people including Loraine's daughter Kayleigh. All of Loraine's children have inherited some psychic ability but it seems particularly strong in Kayleigh. The group gathered at the Ely Cathedral car park and right away Loraine picked up on the spirit of a boy who she claimed had drowned nearby and was following them. She also picked up the spirit of another young man who had died with him, and she told the group that these young men were asking if someone named Dave was present. According to Loraine, these two spirits were very much hoping to connect to an individual named Dave.

Afterwards, Neil discovered that only two weeks before, two young men who were half-brothers, aged 17 and 22, had drowned just five miles away in the nearby Lake Mere at the Kingfishers Bridge Project near Wicken Fen, Cambridgeshire. The news article of this tragic event reported quotes of tribute to these fine young men, including one from the older lad's father whose first name, according to the news, was "Dave."

Loraine "heard" from two young men who had drowned nearby. Neil's investigation revealed a report of two half-brothers who had recently drowned about five miles away. This photo from the Mail Online, 13 September 2011, shows the police search for the two young men.

As Loraine and Neil and the rest of the group continued down the street, Loraine said she was picking up a military connection. Although there was no longer a trace of a military presence, Neil knew that the area had once held a military barracks.

The group continued walking towards Cathedral Green. Just as they neared the cathedral, Loraine picked up the fact that someone had been burned there. She said three people were killed at the same time, but the other two were killed in a different location. Later when Neil investigated her statement, he found that in 1558 there had been three martyrs burned at the stake for heresy. As Loraine had said, one had been killed right there in Cathedral Green, while the other two had been burned at the stake in Oxford.

From the green, the group continued along until they came to an archway called the Porta Gate, which represents the oldest part of the cathedral grounds and dates back to the 13th century. The area still houses members of the clergy.

At this location, Loraine "saw" a woman dressed in a long blue flowing dress and "heard" the name Elizabeth. According to Loraine, this spirit was not an angry spirit but seemed more curious about what they were doing. Neil's later research revealed that a woman named Elizabeth Gauden, now dead, had lived nearby and during her life had made official reports of hauntings she had experienced in the area.

At that point, the mood began to darken. The people on the tour grew quiet and Neil felt inexplicably anxious. Loraine explained that they were being watched by the spirits of several bishops. In the image she saw, they were dressed in red robes with oversized red hats. According to her, the spirits of these ancient bishops weren't pleased with their visitors and didn't appreciate being disturbed. They "told" Loraine she was a heretic and had no business holding a ghost walk on what they considered to be consecrated ground.

As the group continued walking they came to a gate that was normally left open for exit but was locked shut. Instead of retreating the way they had come, the group forged ahead. They hadn't gone far when Loraine stopped and pointed to the brick wall beside them. "There," she said, pointing to the wall. "There is a row of monks holding their hands up, signalling for us to stop. They don't want us to go on."

Neil couldn't see anything on the wall but he felt very uncomfortable. There were no street lights in that area and it was quite dark, and some of the people in the group were afraid to continue.

Neil wasn't about to be stopped by anything, especially something that wasn't physically there, so he went first, leading the group onwards. As he guided the group around a corner, a big gush of air hit him in the chest. He fought his way past it and pressed ahead.

As they walked around to the other side of the cathedral, Loraine said this was where people had worshiped God, but not far away, there had been devil-worshiping. Perhaps, Loraine thought, this might have even involved some type of sacrifice. Neil searched the literature but wasn't able to find anything to corroborate this.

The group returned the way they had come. Although they had not seen any guards or grounds keepers, they found that the exit gate which had been locked before was now open. As they left the green, the group's mood lifted, no longer tense. But as they went out, Loraine's daughter Kayleigh had a strong feeling they were being watched. She didn't see anything but took a picture of where they had just been. The photo she took on her mobile phone showed a faintly glowing image in the distance hovering over a bench they had just left. The image seemed to be wearing a "hat." Kayleigh looked out towards the bench but whatever it was in the photo was not visible to the human eye.

I examined the image on the screen of Kayleigh's phone. It does not seem to have been caused by light filtered from behind the background trees because it comes down too low in the frame. It is not light reflecting off the leaves in the foreground since it occurs further back in the picture in the mid-distance. It isn't a smudge on the lens because it doesn't appear in any of the other photos she took that night before or afterwards. It is simply unexplained.

After they left that area, the group decided to hold hands and conduct a séance. As they concentrated, it seemed to Neil that the night time dusty colour of the grass went gray. He felt

↑

Kayleigh's photo of an unexplained glowing image on
Cathedral Green, Ely

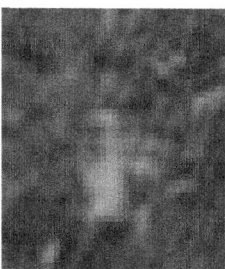

Blow-up of the image

movement against his legs as if the ground was undulating. Others felt it too. Loraine told them the reason they were feeling a sense of movement was because they were passing through the different levels of time. Neil did not see any other images, but Loraine reported what she "saw."

She explained they were in the presence of a German queen who had been treated badly, either by the bishops or the king. Neil believes that could have described Queen Matilda from the 11th century who had been treated badly by those in power. Loraine also noted that there was a male spirit who had joined the group. She claimed this was a modern-day spirit, but the man only had one leg. Neil had not told her that his father, now deceased, had only one leg.

They continued down a side alley to Silver Street where Loraine "saw" the spirit of a woman playing with her children.

From there, they continued towards where Oliver Cromwell had lived and past St Mary's church. At this point, Loraine's daughter Kayleigh "saw" a woman dressed in a wedding gown with her hand up against a tree. The woman's spirit told Kayleigh that she had died just eight days before her wedding and that she had been buried in her bridal gown, which was a 1940's or 1950's style. Neil researched that story but was not able to corroborate it.

By this time, it was getting late so they looped back. They thought the ghost walk was over, but there was one last surprise. As they crossed the street to return to their cars, Loraine said, "I've got somebody else who died here in a traffic crossing. It's an elderly female." Once Neil got home and checked the records, sure enough, within the previous two weeks he discovered there had been a fatality involving an elderly woman at that same zebra crossing where they had been.

CHAPTER 2. THE WISBECH GHOST WALK
October 2011

The third ghost walk was scheduled on 17 October 2011. They decided to hold this event in Wisbech, an area that was new to Neil, who didn't know the town's history.

There were about 15 people on this ghost walk including Neil, Loraine, Kayleigh, and Loraine's son Billy. The group started walking from the town square, one of the oldest sections of town. They came to a very old pub that was closed for renovations. As they looked in the window, Loraine and her son Billy said they could see spirits walking about.

They continued past some residential buildings that had been remodelled into posh flats. Quite a few of the people in the group began to feel sick. Neil got an instant headache. Loraine told them the building had been an old hospital. Later Neil's research showed that the building indeed had been used as an infirmary up until World War I.

The group continued along by a brick wall. Neil felt a distinct presence; and on the brick wall, he thought he saw a window. When he looked again, there was no window, just an ordinary brick wall. It was the first time he saw an image of something that wasn't actually there. He didn't tell anyone what he had seen but he wasn't surprised when Loraine stopped the group and explained that she saw an elderly gent who used to work with his hands, looking out from what had once been a window.

NEIL HUMPHRIES, ghost detective

At this point the group held hands to perform a séance near the church. As they did, the majority of people felt a pain in one leg.

Loraine explained. "Black slaves were manacled here. They were chained together along one leg." Later, Neil's research showed that the slave trade had once been a thriving part of Wisbech. Thomas Clarkson, a local man born in Wisbech in 1760, had spent much of his life protesting the slave trade that saw many black slaves bound for Caribbean plantations come through the ports of Wisbech.

The group proceeded down a very dark alley. Several of the people felt a sense of foreboding and refused to walk down the alley. Neil went in front with Loraine and some of the others followed.

Neil, who had never felt such a strong sense of a presence before the ghost walks, got the unshakeable feeling that someone was watching them. It seemed like a very strong spirit.

Loraine told the group that she felt the presence of a man linked to witches. At that point, Loraine's daughter Kayleigh screamed. She exclaimed that she could see a threatening man and described a man in a tall black hat with a stick in his hand.

Kayleigh felt moved to go into the middle of their circle but Loraine advised against it.

"He's laughing about us being frightened," Loraine said. "I am getting the name Popkins or Hopkins."

Neil told Loraine that the only Hopkins he knew of was Matthew Hopkins, an historic figure who had called himself the Witchfinder General.

"This is him," said Loraine. "He's here, and he took great pleasure in sending witches to their death. He did it with his friend, John."

Neil's research later revealed that Hopkins' main informer and co-conspirator in the witch hunts was John Stearne, a land owner from Lawshall in Suffolk. With John Stearne's assistance, Hopkins used his knowledge of the law at the time including "the Witchcraft Act" to accuse numerous women of witchcraft and send them to their deaths. Between 1644 and 1646, he was responsible for the torture and murder of an estimated 230 women with "proof" as inconsequential as having a birthmark or a pet cat. According to Loraine, some of the victims were as young as nine years old. The historical image Neil found for Matthew Hopkins, with a tall black hat and a cane, was identical to the way Kayleigh had described him.

Oddly enough, Neil's research also revealed that Hopkins, who seems to have died around the age of 28, might have eventually been killed by an angry mob who falsely accused him of witchcraft because they didn't appreciate his meddling with their townswomen.

Neil believes that if they hold a future ghost walk in the Stamford area, Hopkins might likely show up again since the self-appointed Witchfinder General had "worked" there during his life as well. But Neil is not going to mention that to Loraine. Whatever missions they go on in the future, Neil is sure the spirits will speak to Loraine for themselves, and given what she does, he's sure she will have no trouble hearing what they have to say.

Matthew Hopkins, the self-appointed
Witchfinder General who lived
around 1619 - 1647 and terrorized
many communities

CHAPTER 3. A PSYCHIC SKETCH ARTIST

I completed the first book about Loraine in the spring of 2011. As we held our last interview for that book, I got the idea to do a sketch of Loraine's spirit guide, Ramos. When I had first met Loraine years before, I knew she had amazing accuracy, but I didn't really believe that her information was coming through a spirit guide who had lived and died hundreds of years ago as an Egyptian man. I knew Loraine's information was accurate, but I didn't have any idea where it came from. However, during one of Loraine's events, a woman in the audience gasped and then explained that she had seen a presence around Loraine. I spoke to the woman afterwards who described the spirit she saw in the same way that Loraine describes Ramos. After that, I came to accept that Loraine's information really does come from a spirit guide who had once walked the earth as a man named Ramos.

During the final interview session for that first book, as soon as I took out my sketch book to see if I could capture the image of Loraine's spirit guide, I started drawing. I said, "His nose looked like this right? No, wait. It was more like this, wasn't it?" Then I corrected the feature and continued on.

"His forehead was high, like this," I said. "Wait a minute. It was more like this, wasn't it?" Again, I corrected the feature.

This went on for several minutes as I worked on the sketch, adding features, correcting, and adding more features.

After a while, Loraine said, "That's him, all right. But I haven't said hardly anything. You're making this sketch all on your own. How do you know what Ramos looks like? Can you see him?"

"No," I said. "I can't 'see' anything. I'm just drawing."

"I think you're a psychic sketch artist," Loraine told me. "Why don't you come to my next show and see if you can draw the spirits that come through?"

It sounded preposterous to me. How could I draw something I couldn't even see? How could I possibly be a psychic sketch artist? I had never even heard of that before, and found it

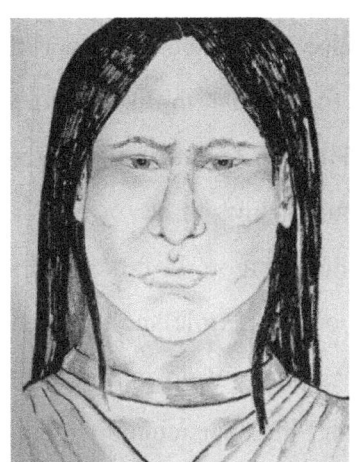

My sketch of Ramos

all pretty hard to believe. But Loraine really wanted me to give it a try, so I agreed to think about it. I was not aware at the time that spending time in the presence of a powerful psychic sometimes triggers or fosters abilities in others that might otherwise have remained dormant.

A few weeks later on 3 March 2011, Loraine conducted a show in Uxbridge, and I went along to see if I could sketch anything. As Loraine began the show, she first came to a woman and started to give her messages that she felt were from the spirit of the woman's departed mother. As soon as Loraine came to that first woman, I drew her as she sat in the audience before me, but I also added a figure behind her of an older woman who was not actually in the room. The shape of the two noses was different and I got the distinct feeling that the woman in the audience must have inherited her nose from her father instead of her mother.

But why would I think that?

As the evening went on, Loraine read about a dozen people. I did a little sketch of the people she read, and in several of those pictures, I added the image of an individual from the spirit world that I felt was "with" that particular person. Of those drawings where I had included a spirit image, several people said that they recognized traits of their departed loved one. One woman told me that I had the hair wrong, but had captured the gaunt features of her dear friend who had died of cancer. The woman was very appreciative to have the sketch, a tangible reminder that her friend's spirit was very much still around her.

Based on the comments and feedback I received that first night, it seemed that I was getting around half of the drawings correct, where the people getting the readings could recognize features on the sketches as having belonged to their loved ones. In a coin toss 50% is not impressive, but this wasn't a coin toss. I was drawing images of faces which could have any number of specific attributes. To find that I had any level of accuracy on something as specific as a likeness of someone who was no longer alive came as quite a shock to me. I was equally surprised that right from the start, it felt comfortable and natural to be drawing images that held great emotional content for total strangers. Unlike giving a speech or a presentation which always gives me an energetic feeling of excitement, this was a calm process that gave me a feeling of quiet connection to something beyond myself. It was an extraordinary experience and completely unexpected.

Since that show, I try to attend Loraine's shows with my sketch book whenever my schedule allows. For the most part, I don't actually "see" the spirit person or get a clear image, although sometimes I do get a clear image in mind. Usually, I have a feeling about a few key features and start with that. Once the sketch takes shape, sometimes the feeling gets stronger, although not always.

Sometimes I miss the mark completely and the person in the audience can't place the image I have drawn at all. I wondered if my accuracy would increase with practice but so far it hasn't. I seem to stay at about the same level, sometimes getting about half of the drawings right, sometimes only one out of four. When I get a particularly strong feeling, those drawings are most likely to be right. It's not a perfect record by any means and not a particularly predictable talent, but when it works it is always rewarding to see the look of astonished delight when my sketches have a special meaning to them.

At that first show I sketched for Loraine, I was so surprised to get anything right that I gave the drawings away without documenting them. I have since learned to photograph them first.

On 25 June 2011, Loraine held a show in Coventry. I did six drawings during the show that included images of spirits. Three of the drawings didn't get positive feedback. For the other three sketches, people found special meaning in the images. I have included these drawings on the following pages, along with the stories behind them.

CHARME AND HER TEDDY-BOY DAD. This was a woman in the audience named Charme whose father came through to Loraine. I had drawn Charme with a man from the spirit world behind her. When I showed her the picture, I asked her if she had any idea what that funny thing on his forehead might be, because I didn't have a clue. She told me, "When he was a young man, my father used to wear his hair in a Teddy-boy style like that."

Sometimes the images I draw are younger than the people were when they died. According to Loraine, the spirits choose how they want to be remembered and might wish to "come through" looking as they did in their prime.

ALISON AND HER GRAN. Here is another example of a spirit choosing how she wanted to be remembered. Alison, the woman wearing the beads in this picture, came to the show with her partner (on her left). Loraine told Alison that her grandmother's spirit was with her. As I sketched a figure behind Alison, I felt that her grandmother had been a much larger woman than the image I was drawing. When Alison saw the picture, she seemed confused. I understood her confusion since I was feeling it, too, as I knew her grandmother had been much larger than the image she was having me draw. The first and only thing I said to Alison was, "But the shawl's right, isn't it? She always wore her shawl, didn't she?"

Alison agreed that her grandmother did like to wear her shawl.

JANE AND HER FATHER-IN-LAW. Loraine did a reading for a woman named Jane who had lost her father. Loraine delivered several messages from him that had special meaning to Jane. I drew a male image from the spirit world to the left of Jane, and assumed it was her father. When Jane saw the picture, she said with surprise, "that's not my father, it's my father-in-law! It's him!"

Jane's father-in-law had also crossed over. A few days later, while reviewing the tapes of that session, I found that Loraine had told Jane that all her relatives were together on the other side. It is interesting that most of the messages Loraine relayed for Jane were from Jane's father while my picture was of her late father-in-law. It does support Loraine's message that all of Jane's relatives were together and wishing to send her special messages and love.

However it happens, I am always glad when it works and the drawing means something to a person, a further reminder that when the body eventually wears out, the soul does not die with it.

CHAPTER 4. CLAIRVOYANT EVENING
AT WALLINGFORD, MARCH 2011

All the spirits who contact Loraine want something; however, as can be seen in the previous chapter, not all are troubled by negative feelings or violence. The great majority of insistent spirits who come through to Loraine at her readings and shows make their presence known out of concern for their loved ones still on Earth. The primary focus for these gentle souls is to deliver messages of comfort and confirmation.

I brought my sketchbook to another show Loraine held, on 3 March 2012, at the Portcullis Club in Wallingford, near Oxford. As the event started, Loraine introduced baby Ollie who had been born premature but was doing well now thanks to the excellent medical care he received at the Special Care Baby Unit at the John

Radcliffe Hospital. The event was coordinated by Ollie's grandmother Mandy, who had helped Loraine set up the evening. As Loraine explained, the proceeds of the night were to go to the Special Care Baby Unit to support the hospital. Loraine also mentioned to the audience that a portion of the sale from every copy of her book goes to the Great Ormond Street hospital in London, another worthy charity that Loraine endorses.

LORAINE WITH MANDY at the Wallingford fundraiser event.

The first person in the audience Loraine came to that evening was a young man named Chris. Loraine told him he was a really nice person who tries to please everyone and that his grandfather comes around him often.

Loraine asked him, "Who has trouble with their eyes?"

Chris confirmed that he has problems with his eyes. Loraine told him that it wasn't anything too serious and that he wasn't going to go blind. In fact, she said, "You're going to be looking at yourself in the morning for a long time. Which isn't such a bad thing. You could be looking at me tomorrow night."

Chris and the audience appreciated the levity and the evening was off to a flying start.

Loraine told Chris that although he loves his partner very much, they do peeve each other. She also told Chris she was getting a message from his grandmother who wanted to assure him that things would start to look up financially for him.

Loraine asked, "Who had the cancer?" Chris confirmed that it was indeed his grandmother who had died from cancer.

Loraine asked him who had lost his dog, and Chris confirmed that he had lost his dog. Loraine wound up the reading by telling Chris his grandmother was being very insistent that his finances would be changing for the better very soon.

As Loraine gave Chris these messages, I drew him with the image of an older woman above him.

CHRIS and the woman I drew above him.

Loraine's shows usually include a break halfway through, and during the break, I showed Chris the sketch and asked him if it was his grandmother.

He looked at me in surprise and exclaimed, "That's not my Gran, it's my Dad's sister!" As I have said before, I am not sure how it works. I can only be glad when it does.

Later in the evening, Loraine came to a mother and daughter named Pam and Jess. Loraine gave them several messages from Pam's mother (the grandmother of Jess) who had crossed over. Loraine knew that the woman had died of lung cancer and needed oxygen at the end. As Loraine spoke to Pam and Jess, I sketched them with a pretty young woman behind them wearing her hair in a ponytail held back in a clip.

PAM (left), JESS (right), and the girl I drew behind them

After the reading, I showed them the picture and asked Pam if the girl looked familiar to her.

"My mother was young at heart," Pam told me. "She had long hair like that when she was young, and she always liked it nice and neat. Even at the end when she was very frail, she always had her hair done up very neat and pretty."

PAM AND JESS examine the sketch. "As a girl, my mother had long hair like that."

One of the people who received a reading that night was a woman named Jane. Loraine told Jane that her grandmother on her maternal side was there, a woman who had lovely skin when she was alive. Loraine also said that Jane's mother, still alive, would be moaning and groaning at least another ten years and would live to be a very old woman. Loraine confided that Jane's mother likes to pretend she's deaf, but she can actually hear everything that's going on very well. Jane thought that was funny but also probably true.

Loraine asked who had the heart attack, and Jane replied that it was her dad's brother who had died three weeks ago. Loraine said that the man was very much loved and that no one had a bad word to say about him at his funeral. She also told Jane that her uncle knew this year would be his last Christmas and, in his own way, had said goodbye at the festivities.

Loraine saw that Jane had experienced three deaths in the family that were all very sudden. Jane agreed that this was true.

Loraine asked who was named Ted or Edward. Jane explained that it was her husband's father. Loraine told her that her entire family was all together on the other side.

Loraine "saw" Jane's late husband, and said that he had been very handsome in his day. "Why is he telling me he's sorry?" Loraine asked.

Jane nodded. "I understand that."

Loraine said, "He had some regrets, but he loved you loads. He says that he *knows* and it's okay to be angry with him."

This made perfect sense to Jane.

My drawing of Jane contained a woman in the background.

JANE (front) and a very free spirit image with wind in her hair.

I asked Jane if she knew who the woman might be, and she was pleased that it looked like her mother-in-law, now deceased. As Loraine had told Jane, her family was all together on the other side, and Jane was glad to see the drawing of her mother-in-law looking so content and at peace.

* * *

During that show, Loraine explained that when we die, we retain our feelings and emotions. She said that those in the spirit world miss us as much as we miss them, even though they can still see us and observe what we do.

Then she went on to tell a few stories about the trials and tribulations of being a medium and the outrageous experiences that would be hard to make up.

One time Loraine was invited to give a mediumship demonstration on a pavilion stage. As Loraine was announced and came onto the stage, her attention was drawn to a girl in the crowd who was about 26 years old. Loraine knew that the girl had recently lost her mother because she was feeling a very strong mothering energy around her.

"I have your mum here," Loraine told the girl.

"You can't," said the girl, confused.

"She's definitely saying that she's your mother," Loraine answered.

The girl replied, "That's not possible."

"Why is that?" Loraine asked.

The girl answered, "Because my mother's dead."

* * *

Another time, Loraine met a woman, about 38 years old, who was dressed in a very posh outfit with carefully layered strands of gold jewellery. Loraine immediately felt the presence of a man who was so old that Loraine at first assumed he was the woman's father. That is, until the old gent's spirit "spoke" to Loraine and told her, "That's my wife."

Loraine turned to the woman. "I've got your husband here."

The woman folded her arms. "I don't want to speak with him."

In her mind, Loraine heard the old boy's spirit say, "Of course she doesn't want to speak with me. She killed me."

Loraine debated a moment if she should relay this particular message. Of course, she knew it could land her in hot water. But as a translator, Loraine feels that it is her job to deliver the message and not censor it. This occasionally gets her into trouble but she feels that in order to honour the process, she has to honour the message she receives no matter how outlandish it sounds.

When Loraine relayed the message, the woman wasn't shocked or offended. Instead, she confided: "I didn't really kill him. I only stopped his medication because I didn't like him anymore."

* * *

Just as Loraine never knows what a spirit person will tell her, she never knows what a living person is going to say or do when she starts a reading. At one demonstration she conducted in Croydon, a man came in wearing a dress and told her that he had left his wife and had changed his name to Karen. Right away, Loraine got a message from his deceased father.

"I've got your dad here," she said, "and I'm hearing the name *Paul*."

"That was my name before the sex change," the fellow told Loraine, lifting his skirt. "But it's not complete yet because I've still got *THAT*."

Two years later, Loraine was back doing another show in the town, and the same person came running up to her, breathless with news and skirt flapping.

"It's me, Karen! I'm a FULL woman now. Look!"

Loraine shook her head. "Karen, I have to say I'm a bit confused. I see that you've had the change, but for some reason, I still see you with a woman."

Karen nodded happily. "That's because I've gone back to my wife. We're lesbians!"

* * *

The last person Loraine read at the Wallingford show was a woman named Pat. Loraine saw quite a few spirits around Pat, and asked Pat if she had experienced a lot of losses lately. Pat agreed that this was true.

Loraine felt a strong father link around Pat, and asked if someone had been having trouble with their toes.

"My daughter," Pat explained.

Loraine got the image of someone who loved his garden and played the piano. He even fancied himself a singer although even he had to admit that in life, he had a terrible voice.

Pat nodded at that.

Then Loraine told Pat that her husband would have been 70 if he was still living. She went on to say that Pat's father had died at a very young age (Pat confirmed he died at age 24), which was why Pat ended up being the baby of her family.

Loraine told Pat that her brother didn't want to leave but he had no choice. Then she asked who died of bowel cancer, and Pat explained that it was her grandmother.

Loraine assured Pat that although she had already experienced more than her fair share of being the funeral queen, there would be no more deaths in her family for a while. Pat was greatly relieved to hear that.

While Loraine was doing the reading, I drew an image of Pat with a man behind her with a long nose and chin. I assumed it was her father, because Loraine had spoken of a father link.

PAT and the male figure behind her

When I showed Pat the drawing, she didn't say anything for a moment but asked me if she could show it to her daughter. Her daughter, who was sitting on the other side of the room, came over and looked at it with her mother.

Then Pat pulled out a picture she had folded up in her pocket. The photo was of a man with a long face and curly hair that looked very much like my drawing.

"That's your answer," she said. "It's my brother."

"Did you come here hoping to hear from him?" I asked.

"Yes," she said. "I only went to my brother's funeral Wednesday. That's him, all right, without his glasses. It's amazing. I put this picture of him in my pocket before I came. Nobody knew I had it with me. He had cancer. It had spread all

PAT'S BROTHER ART
This is the photo Pat brought in her pocket
to Loraine's show, hoping to get a message from him.

through him. He loved his garden, just as Loraine said. She couldn't have possibly known I was the baby of the family." This was the first time anyone had pulled out a photograph of someone I had drawn on a feeling. Although Pat's photo was a folded colour Xerox copy and my picture was a simple sketch, the similarities were striking.

As I compared the drawing with the photo, I noticed something I hadn't realized before.

"I've made his head bigger than yours," I told Pat. "Usually, when I draw from a feeling, the images are the same size or smaller than the people actually in front of me. But in this case, I drew his face larger than yours. He must have been a very big presence."

Pat nodded. "He was the only one in the family with curly hair," she said, "and that's just how you've drawn him. He was an artist and a musician, but he couldn't sing."

"So *that's* what Loraine was talking about," I said.

"My husband would have been 70 this month," Pat explained. "Loraine was damned accurate on all counts. I've lost two brothers and my son, then my other brother in December, and then Art after that. Loraine was too accurate. It's been a hard few years and I'm glad to think there will be no more deaths for a while."

I asked, "Does it help to hear that they are still around?"

Pat told me, "I've always known they're still around me. I can feel them here. Before my husband crossed, he had seen my son, who was gone by then, on a couple of occasions. Sometimes he even felt a little kick from beyond."

Pat believes there is a blueprint of our lives and that our deaths are predestined. However it happens, she was relieved to hear Loraine say that there may be no more funerals for her on the horizon.

Pat gave me the folded page with her brother's image that she had carried in her pocket. It was from her brother's funeral service, and below his picture a poem was printed that gave a moving tribute to this special soul. In celebration of that life and of the generous spirit who somehow made his image so clear to me, I am pleased to share this poem about the bonds of love and the beauty of a treasured life.

You can shed tears that he has gone,
Or you can smile because he has lived.
You can close your eyes and pray that he'll come back,
Or you can open your eyes and see all that he has left.

Your heart can be empty because you cannot see him,
Or you can be full of the love that you have shared.
You can turn your back on tomorrow and live for yesterday,
Or you can be happy for tomorrow because of yesterday.

You can remember him and ache that he has gone,
Or you can cherish his memory and let him live on.
You can cry and close your mind, be empty and turn your back,
Or you can do what he would want -- smile, open your eyes,
love and go on.

CHAPTER 5. THE HORNCHURCH SHOW
23 March 2012

On the evening of 23 March, Loraine held a show in Hornchurch in Essex. Since Loraine is from Essex, a number of people who had known her a long time were planning to come. I arrived early to speak to as many of her long-time friends as I could before the show began.

I started by interviewing Diane, a woman who has worked for Loraine scheduling her bookings.

Diane met Loraine years ago before Loraine had begun to work as a psychic. In those days, Loraine used to come to Diane's house and do informal readings for friends and family. Back then,

Loraine didn't have tarot cards or anything to help her. All she used was a pack of regular playing cards. But even using that simple deck of playing cards, Loraine was able to tell Diane things she shouldn't have possibly known.

Still, Diane was sceptical and held onto her disbelief for a while. This came to an abrupt halt one day when Diane and her sister Carol stopped by to visit Loraine. That day, Loraine held up a chain and told them they could ask questions and she would get an answer for them, depending on whether the pendulum moved sideways, round and round, or didn't move at all.

Loraine held up the chain and told Diane to ask a question. Once Diane asked her question, the chain started swinging.

"Of course it's moving," said Diane. "You're doing it. It's nothing more than mind over matter. Your hand is making the chain move. It's nothing special, it's just gravity."

Loraine told Diane to hold the chain herself.

"Then it will be *my* hand that will move it with gentle vibrations," Diane responded. "It's got nothing to do with hocus pocus or anything like that."

"All right then," said Loraine. "Just hold the chain and watch this."

Carol held the chain up as Diane observed, feeling confident that nothing Loraine could do would change her mind.

Loraine said out loud, "Okay, Ramos. I want you to show these girls how tactful you are. I want you to move the chain out to the side and then back to the centre."

Diane said, "That can't happen."

But as she watched the chain in her sister's hand, it did. The bottom of the chain moved two inches to the right side. Then instead of swinging back to the opposite side, as it should have, it went back to the centre and just stopped dead.

Carol, who was holding the chain, was so startled that she stood up and threw the chain across the room.

From that point on, Diane and Carol had no choice but to believe that Loraine was genuinely linking with energy that was connected beyond the physical world.

A few years later, Diane discovered her husband had been cheating. After she had left him, Diane met up with Loraine, who gave Diane the names of a number of women. Diane checked it out and found out that Loraine was right on all counts.

As Diane explains it, whenever she starts to doubt Loraine's talent, Loraine does something that once again makes it impossible to disbelieve. A few years after the pendulum incident, Diane began working for Loraine arranging her bookings. One

DIANE (standing) AND HER SISTER CAROL (seated) take tickets at the Hornchurch show. The sisters used to be sceptics.

afternoon, Loraine did a reading for Diane and said she was getting a message for Diane from a young woman in Australia. Diane had a cousin in Australia but had only met her once, as a very young girl, and didn't even know her cousin's real name. She knew her cousin by a nickname only, but didn't share it with Loraine.

Loraine told Diane that she was very clearly getting a

message about someone in Australia whose name began with the letter "I", and thought it might be Iris or Irene. Loraine felt it was about a young woman who was still on the Earth plane.

Diane said, "My aunt's name was Iris."

"No," said Loraine. "This is a younger woman, and not your aunt."

Diane said, "I don't know anyone else with that name."

Loraine said, "All right then. It's Babs."

Diane was stunned. This was the nickname she had used for her distant cousin in Australia. She had only met her once when they were children and had no reason to talk about her or even think about her. Babs wasn't exactly a common name for Loraine to have guessed.

Loraine continued. "You know her as Babs, but her real name is Iris, like her mother's."

Diane denied it. But when she went home and checked with her mother, she was surprised to find out that it was true. Two days later, Diane received an unexpected latter from Iris, the first letter she had ever received from her Australian cousin who wanted to ask Diane if she believed in clairvoyance. Apparently Iris seemed to feel there was a special reason to ask, and couldn't possibly have known that Diane had just begun working for Loraine, scheduling appointments on that exact subject.

* * *

After I spoke with Diane, I met two other sisters, Joanna and Shelly. Joanna had first met Loraine at a girlie weekend away in Blackpool when they were in their early twenties. At that time, Loraine gave all the girls on the weekend trip a reading. Joanna remembered the predictions, and was stunned when all of them eventually came true, from the colour of her first car to the traits of her partner. Loraine also told Joanna that she was going to meet a man with brown eyes and live abroad.

"Not me," said Joanna.

"I'm seeing you living in Spain," Loraine told her.

Years later, Joanna's sister Shelly met a man with dark eyes and moved with him to Spain.

"This has happened before," said Joanna. "A psychic might get the situation right, but the message might be for my sister, and not actually for me."

I had to agree. I had seen two other instances where Loraine predicted a specific situation that came true not for the person she indicated but instead happened to someone very close to them.

Joanne didn't see Loraine again until years later when she went to a show in Upminster. She was delighted to see that the featured medium up on the stage was Loraine.

During the show, Loraine came to Joanna's mother, who Loraine had never met before. Loraine said, "I'm seeing the Isle of Dogs."

Joanna's mother was surprised because she had grown up on the Isle of Dogs. She wasn't at all prepared when Loraine continued with, "Why am I getting Glengall Road?"

Joanna and her mother gasped because that was the name of the street where Joanna's mother had lived as a child.

Loraine also gave her some names of departed loved ones that she felt were around her. The names turned out to be the father of Joanna's mum and also the grandfather. Loraine said the last one had been in the military as she was getting the feeling of a soldier standing at attention. This was confirmed -- Joanna's great-grandfather had been a soldier.

A few years later, Joanna's sister Shelly had a reading with Loraine. Shelly was married at the time and Loraine told her some things about her husband that Shelly dearly hoped were not true. Unfortunately, Shelly discovered that these things were true after all and had to face the sad fact that her husband wasn't the man

JOANNE (left) AND HER SISTER SHELLY never know
what Loraine will surprise them with next.

she trusted him to be.

Whether the message is good news or not, Joanna and Shelly are glad to get whatever message Loraine has for them and are pleased to come see her whenever they can.

Loraine does not censor herself and will deliver whatever message she gets. As a medium, she feels that it is her job to be a conduit and deliver the message that comes to her, without censorship or alteration. Just like a conscientious translator wouldn't dream of changing a message to suit his or her own agenda or morals, Loraine delivers the message as accurately as she can.

Not everyone appreciates Loraine's honesty. While writing

this book, I met a man training to be a medium who was outraged to hear that Loraine delivers messages that are not always favourable. He insisted that there were boundaries on what a medium should or shouldn't say. He felt that mediums were morally obligated to interfere with a message and disregard it if it didn't fit with his own personal values and views. It seems that the spirits didn't agree with his thoughts on editing their messages as he never received any. After his repeated efforts to connect to the other side ended in failure, he ended up dropping out of mediumship school.

* * *

Before the show started I also talked with Julie, another long time friend of Loraine's. Loraine and Julie had first met on a cruise many years before. On the cruise, Loraine told Julie that she would fall pregnant with twins. A few months later, Loraine phoned Julie and asked, "Are you pregnant yet?"

"You were right," said Julie. "I am pregnant. I just came back from the doctor and had my 12th week scan. And you were right about one other thing -- it's twins."

They kept in touch over the phone as Julie's pregnancy progressed. Then one day, Loraine called Julie on the phone.

"There's something wrong with your babies," Loraine said.

"How can that be?" Julie asked. "I just went to the doctor's yesterday and he said everything was fine."

"Go again," Loraine told her. "Go now! If those babies aren't born today, they won't survive."

Julie was still five weeks away from her due date but went to her doctor and told him she was concerned that something might be wrong. She didn't tell him why she was concerned; she only asked him if he would check.

The doctor did a foetal heart scan and discovered that the

JULIE (left) AND HER DAUGHTER at the Hornchurch show
If Loraine hadn't warned her, Julie's twin sons would have both died.
Instead, they were delivered just in time.

heartbeats of her unborn sons were dangerously weak. The hospital rushed Julie into the operating room right away. It was touch and go for a while. One of the twins was clinically dead when he was born but the doctors were able to revive him and both babies survived. The doctor told Julie that if she hadn't

come in when she had, she would have lost both of her sons.

* * *

At 7:30 PM, Loraine starts the show. The second person she comes to is a woman named Mandy. Loraine explains that Mandy has lost her father because she's picking up a dad link. Mandy agrees that this is true.

"You really feel robbed of his life," Loraine says. "He tells me that you feel lonely sometimes even when there are other people around. Your mother's still alive, isn't she? He's telling me that she's still on the Earth plane, whining and moaning."

Mandy confirms that her mother is still here.

Loraine says, "But she's not in the room tonight, is she?"

Mandy shakes her head.

"Your father says it's a good thing she didn't hear him say that, because he was in enough trouble with your mum when he was alive. Now, if I said the name John, would you know who this is?"

Mandy does.

"How about Albert or Bertie?"

Mandy recognizes that name as well.

Loraine has walked down the edge of the room and is standing near Mandy, not far from the room's second set of blinds.

"Somebody went to war and never came home," Loraine says. "And your father is telling me that you're not going to die young but will live a long time. Your dad is getting very emotional. He is telling me that he wanted to stay alive and that he really didn't want to go. Now, who is thinking of getting a tattoo?"

As Loraine says this, the window shade near Mandy moves suddenly and the people in the room gasp in surprise. It isn't the gentle shifting in the breeze; it is a circular impact as if someone punched a fist into it from the other side.

But there is no one on the other side of the window.

The entire audience, nearly 150 people, has seen this sudden burst of energy but no one can explain it.

Loraine has said before that spirit is nothing more than energy, and that energy can manifest in different ways.

A murmur grows as people talk to each other about the phenomenon they have all just witnessed.

Loraine says, "There are a lot of lights in this room and a lot of messages for other people to get, so let's keep going."

People quiet down and Loraine continues.

LORAINE AT THE HORNCHURCH SHOW
During the show, the second set of widow shades on the left moved in a way that couldn't be explained. There was no one outside the window.

"Who is thinking of getting a tattoo?" Loraine asks Mandy again.

Mandy confides that she is considering the idea.

Loraine tells her, "Your father doesn't like that idea and he doesn't want you to do it. He says you shouldn't do that to your lovely body and that a lady should be a lady. And with that, I'll leave you with his love and say God bless."

* * *

During the Hornchurch show, I drew four sketches. After the Wallingford show in Oxford where I had sketched Pat's brother Art so accurately, I was thinking that maybe I might be in for another successful sketching night. I did have some success but it was limited. Of the four psychic sketches I drew that night, only one got positive feedback.

It was on the sketch I did of Mandy during the one reading that night where unexplained energy manifested itself in the movement of the window shade. On the sketch of Mandy, I included a father-like figure behind her. I wrote one word on that sketch next to the man's image -- "sideburns." Neither Loraine nor Mandy had mentioned anything about sideburns, but I had a feeling about them that was so strong that I included that word on the sketch. When I showed Mandy the picture I had drawn, I said, "Your father had sideburns, didn't he?"

"Yes," she said, looking at the drawing. "And bushy

MANDY and the father-figure image with the sideburns

eyebrows. This could be him."

At least I got one drawing right that evening.

Sometimes I get a strong feeling. With Mandy's father, the idea of sideburns was insistent enough for me to write the word down on the page. On one of Loraine's ghost walks, I also got particularly strong imagery.

At other times, I get a faint sense of something. If I get any feeling at all of an image, I draw it. Someone asked me why I don't just draw the strong feelings and ignore the weak ones but I don't think that would work. If I started second-guessing myself, wondering and worrying about the strength of the feeling in order to increase my accuracy rate, I think that would get in the way of letting the feelings come. Denying or self-editing any part of the process might block the little wisps and whispers of images that do manage to come my way.

Loraine has always claimed that most people have some psychic ability. Have you ever felt the presence of a departed loved one? Have you thought about a person you hadn't seen in a while and then from out of the blue, received a letter or a phone call from him? Have you ever dreamed of something that came true? As children we tend to exhibit psychic tendencies but as we grow and focus on other things, we often lose touch with those gifts.

When Loraine's parents became aware of the psychic talent she displayed at a very young age, they were surprised by the strength of her ability to link to the spirit world, but not that she could. Coming from a long line of psychicly talented generations of Romany stock, both of her parents had some psychic abilities. When they saw that their young daughter was communicating with spirits so easily, they did not try to dissuade her or tell her she was just being silly; they just accepted it as a fact of her life.

Loraine feels that with guidance and practice, many more people would be able to develop their own inner talents whatever their particular gifts might be.

Some people are clairvoyant, with the ability to see or get images well beyond the normal senses. Others are clairaudient and can hear things in their minds. Still others are clairsentient and can feel what the spirits feel or felt. Loraine links into the spirit world in all three ways.

There are dozens of other paranormal abilities and phenomenon (see the Glossary of Parapsychology Terms at the end of the book). You could be surprised to discover that you have hidden talents. Some people are gifted healers while others are naturally good with animals. There are those who can often predict the sex of a baby or can find things. I have a friend Lisa who always manages to find a parking spot. No matter how crowded the lot is, a space always opens up for her. She confided to me that at times she feels the presence of her ancestors, fiercely devoted to family and still looking out for her. Whenever we go somewhere, I love it when she drives.

You might, like me, discover you have an ability you had never considered or hadn't even heard of.

Incidentally, some time after I began to do psychic sketches for Loraine, I learned that my nephew, who I hadn't seen in years, had started to do "spiritual drawings" for his friends. One drawing held such meaning to a friend that he was moved to tears. As Loraine inherited her strong psychic talent from her family, it may be that my occasional ability to connect through drawing also runs in mine.

In the spring of 2011, Loraine held a psychic development class up near Peterborough. In that session she used guided imagery of a scenic and peaceful landscape. The participants were instructed to close their eyes, take a mental journey, and "meet" their spirit guides. Of the ten people who were there, four people described "seeing" the same vision of young girls in white dresses and flowers in their hair dancing around a ring. Two other participants from opposite sides of the room who had never met before linked into a shared image of a man in dark robes with a wide-brimmed hat with a round top. In other words, over half of the participants experienced collective or shared imagery that overlapped with other participants.

Perhaps, as Loraine contends, most of us do have some degree of psychic ability hidden away deep within us. Perhaps as our society slowly accepts that psychic links exist that defy current explanation, we may be better situated to embrace our spirituality.

In the meantime, I take comfort knowing that there are those rare people in the world like Loraine who can so effortlessly and reliably connect with the world beyond this one. Through the information and details that she provides with such accuracy, it is good to see and hear tangible evidence that our Earthly lives are not all that we are.

CHAPTER 6. DEBUNKING DISBELIEF

I am occasionally asked why a classically trained scientist like me would believe in the spirit world or accept that Loraine can do what I have seen her do repeatedly. I have considered this question carefully and have come up with a few thoughts.

Our technology today can do things that we could not have imagined even a few years ago. Things once considered impossible can quickly become commonplace. New scientific findings and discoveries are being reported every day as we continue to learn about our world and the particles from which it is made.

A medieval person would have had great difficulty accepting the concept of invisible energy waves that could carry messages. What would such a person have thought about the idea of radio waves or mobile phones? Do you think you could convince such a person that this was possible? Perhaps you could if you showed him a mobile phone or a radio. As a species, we love our gadgets. But why is it so much harder to believe in something vastly more complicated -- the untapped potential and diversity of the human mind?

In every field of human endeavour, there are geniuses -- people who have an innate ability to excel beyond their peers at particular tasks or subjects. Is it really so hard to accept that this could apply to psychic abilities as well?

People living in the middle ages would have been told that the Earth is flat. Their wisest scholars believed it; everyone they knew believed it. But what would they think if they climbed a tall mountain and looked out and saw a slight curvature on the Earth's horizon? Would they doubt their eyes? Would they ignore the evidence right before them just because the authorities of their day told them it wasn't possible?

In a way, when I am watching Loraine at work, I feel like an ancient mountain climber staring out at the curvature of the Earth. I am facing direct and tangible evidence through what I have seen and heard that there is more to the soul than the physical world. To ignore the evidence I have witnessed in order to conform to a rigidly held view is the opposite of good science and veers into the realm of doctrine.

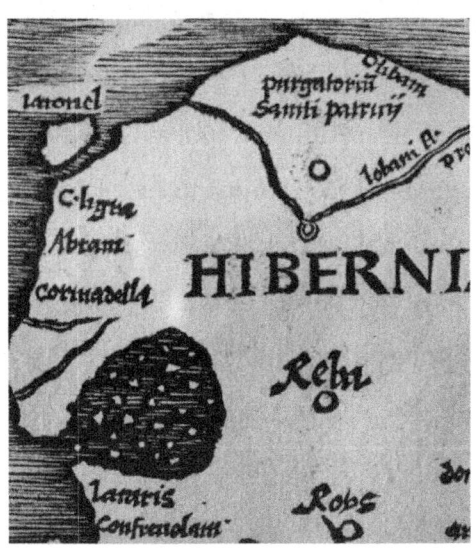

AN ANCIENT MAP OF IRELAND
They didn't know what lay further north so they labelled the top of the map Purgatory. They hadn't been further north so they didn't think anything could exist beyond it. Today there are those who believe that nothing could exist beyond death because they haven't been there -- at least, not yet.

Real science is not about accepting what other people think or tell you to believe, it requires considering the question for yourself using all the information possible. It is not about denying evidence to fit a preconceived or convenient point of view.

Science makes no judgement on what should or shouldn't be believed. Instead, its purpose is to explore and examine what can be seen, recorded, measured, or understood. To make scientific discoveries requires an original thinker and one with a sceptical but open mind. If you told a truly great scientist that the speed of light could be exceeded, he would not say, "It isn't possible." He would say, "Show me. Prove it."

For someone who does not blindly believe doctrine but can think for himself, that is the challenge.

Science also stipulates we should not be rigid in our beliefs but allow them to change as new information arises. Watching Loraine, my conception of what isn't possible is continuously being challenged.

There are those who feel they should deny the existence of the spirit world on the basis of "science." But the truth is that there are very few scientists exploring the question of the spirit world. It is not a typical field of study for scientific experiments. As such, modern science has done little to further our understanding of the soul one way or the other. Ghost hunters use simple recording devices that sometimes document fluctuations or readings that can't always be explained, but these are generally not considered to be scientific experiments. Given the number of fakes out there, it is hard to know what is true.

Perhaps we should look at what we do know.

According to particle physics, some particles have matter, some transmit mass to other particles, while others transmit force. Some particles are postulated to derive their mass by interacting with themselves, and in this complicated arrangement of what various particles do, new particles (and theories) are being discovered and put forth at nuclear colliders. On the larger end of the scale, emerging theories suggest the universe is held together by invisible threads of dark matter that do not react with electromagnetic forces and are at present poorly understood. Clearly there is much we don't know about the intricacies of the particles that make up our world and the forces that shape what those pieces do and how they relate.

Modern science postulates that energy does not cease to exist, it is instead converted to another form. We know that humans emit electromagnetic radiation. What happens to that energy when we die?

I once met a woman who was such a strong conductor of electromagnetic energy that she had been hit by lightning twice. She seemed to be a natural magnet for lightning. The only other person I have ever heard of being struck twice by lightning was her father.

Just as some individuals may be naturally strong conduits for electrical energy, is it too much to consider that perhaps some people are genetically predisposed to be better conduits for spiritual energy?

Loraine's readings are hard to ignore. The specificity and accuracy of her information is well beyond clever guessing. As neurosurgeon Dr. Hisham Daghestani says, "The spiritual phenomenon displayed by Loraine Rees cannot be explained. Her high level of accuracy and specificity defies orthodox scientific methodology."

If we want to consider the question of spiritual connectivity scientifically, we can look at the few scientists who *are* studying it with scientific rigor.

One of the leading scientists in the field of parapsychology, Dr. Gary Schwartz, has conducted numerous studies on the subject (see a list of his books in Appendix C). While Loraine has not been involved with his experiments, he has used respected mediums with a talent level similar to Loraine's, with an accuracy rating of 80% or more. His tests use rigorous scientific techniques where "double blind" methods are involved. This means that the person asking the questions doesn't know the answer to ensure that he or she is not inadvertently "signalling" information to the person being tested. According to Dr. Swartz's results, the accuracy of specific information recorded in these sessions that these mediums have provided is statistically valid. His groundbreaking research, the first experiments to explore the question of spiritual connectivity with rigorous scientific principles, is demonstrating the validity of information transfer beyond the physical world. In other words, using scientific scrutiny, his carefully documented work is proving the existence of a world beyond our own -- the existence of a spiritual world.

Not all scientists appreciate the topic of Dr. Swartz's research. There has been a taboo against studying this topic scientifically -- a sort of backwards logic that *if we don't study it, then it can't be true.* That is hardly good science. It is never easy to be the leader in an unconventional field. While Dr. Schwartz is not always appreciated for his choice of research, the scientific rigor he applies to his studies is hard to fault, as are his findings. As more work is done in this radical field using scientific principles, who knows what we will discover.

In the meantime, I will be content to be like the ancient mountain climber gazing out upon the slight curvature of the horizon. I may not understand all the why's and how's of what I am seeing, but as I look out and gaze with wonder at what I have glimpsed, I cannot deny the view.

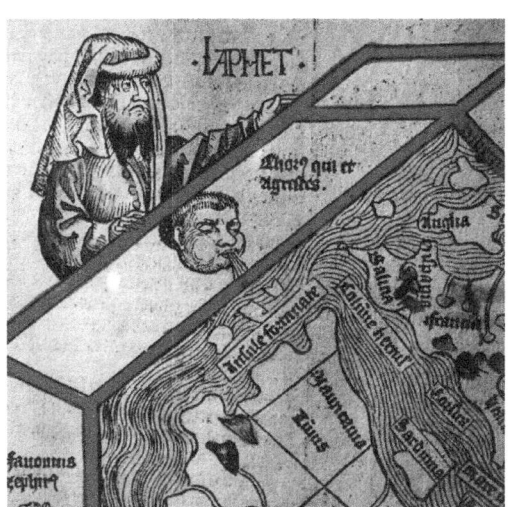

AN ANCIENT MAP OF THE 'FLAT EARTH.'
What do you put at the border of your flat Earth? You could try the west wind and a wise old man holding up the ocean. Will future people look back at our current parapsychology infancy and smile?

CHAPTER 7. NEWBURY

The next show I attended with Loraine occurred several months later in Newbury (September, 2012). It was a packed hall with dozens of people expectantly waiting to see if Loraine would come to them. As Loraine walked around the room, she did several readings, offering specifics and details that could not be denied or otherwise explained. I did a handful of drawings and the features of two of the drawings had special meaning to those being read. All in all, it was what I have come to expect from a typical Loraine Rees clairvoyant event.

One of the more unusual things I encountered at that show was a photograph one of the audience members showed me. Debbie, a new grandmother, recently had a professional photo session taken of her daughter's family. It was an outdoor setting with Debbie's daughter relaxing on a green, grassy lawn with her fiancé and their toddler son who seemed pleased with himself as he took his tenuous steps on the grass.

When Debbie picked up the photographs from the studio, she was surprised to see a sort of gray cloud that appeared on one shot in the background above her daughter. It was not a normal passing cloud since it was not on any of the other pictures in the series. Unlike the green trees around, on the colour shot it is gray, the same colour Loraine and many others see spirits. But the strangest thing about this "cloud" is that it appears in the shape of a face, specifically one that bears a resemblance to Debbie's deceased grandmother, Lillian.

Debbie wanted to know what Loraine thought of the picture and what it might mean. Loraine has seen other unusual photographic images, especially during her ghost walks. She says spirits can sometimes manifest on photographs, usually as gray shapes or patches of light. Other times, their energy appears as orbs (as in Chapter 8). Loraine felt that this was a particularly clear image given from beyond, a reminder of a caring presence that, despite death, was still connected with Debbie and her family.

I've considered the possibilities from all angles. Debbie herself is not trained at creating images; if she was, she wouldn't have had to send her daughter to a professional photographer. The photography studio would have no reason to alter the image and would not have known what Debbie's grandmother looked like. This leaves two options: either a smudge shaped like a face accidentally appeared on the professional photographer's lens for exactly one frame and then disappeared, or that the camera actually recorded Debbie's grandmother's presence, still lovingly connected to her family's joy and special moments. I know which scenario makes the most sense to me.

With Debbie's permission, I have included the picture along with a vintage shot of her grandmother so you can draw your own conclusions.

DEBBIE'S DAUGHTER WITH THE FAMILY. The gray shape above her shoulder does not appear in any of the other frames.

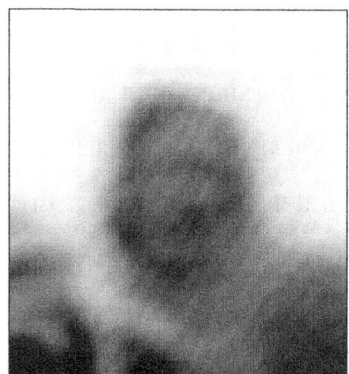

Enlargement of the shape

Debbie's grandmother Lillian,
at an earlier moment of family joy

I have known Loraine for a number of years now, and sometimes I forget what a shock it is to people when they first encounter her and watch her connect with the other side. Even people who would like to think that there is more than this world can find it startling when they meet Loraine and come face to face with evidence that an afterlife exists.

I heard from a woman named Jane who reminded me what it was like to be taken from a mild curiosity about the possibility of an afterlife to stunned conviction.

Jane had first encountered Loraine at a show in Colchester. At the time, Jane was attending a Mind Body Soul event with her sister and mother.

Loraine's session was held in a large room with a few hundred people filling up the seats. Jane and her group were seated near the back as Loraine began her chatty routine, putting the audience at ease and making people laugh.

After a while Loraine said she wanted to go to a woman in the front two rows and honed in on a particular person. Jane couldn't see who Loraine was talking to as she was seated near the back.

Loraine told the woman that her sister had died in an act of violence, and her spirit was still angry about her death. Loraine felt the sister had been stabbed by her boyfriend, and had not died quickly. Instead, the woman had been frightened, and the death had been drawn out.

Loraine iterated that she was not saying this to upset the woman and didn't think she was telling her anything that the police hadn't already told her.

Jane could feel the audience was horrified by the poor spirit's stabbing. Jane was feeling a little horrified, too. But as the reading went on, Jane realized that something about the story seemed familiar.

Jane whispered to her mum, "This sounds like someone I knew." In fact, it sounded like a girl from her school. Although they had been in the same grade, they had travelled in different circles and Jane didn't know the girl very well. Later, she had met the girl's sister at work, and she learned that her old schoolmate was engaged and about to go on holiday with her boyfriend. Jane was pleased for her. But about a year after that, Jane was shocked to learn that her old schoolmate had been killed by her boyfriend.

Could Loraine really be communicating with the spirit of someone Jane had actually known?

Loraine wrapped up the reading and the session ended. As people started to leave the hall, Jane asked her mum and her sister to wait a few minutes. She just had to see who received that reading. Could it really be her old schoolmate's sister?

As the crowd took their leave and the people from the front finally made their way out, Jane was stunned to see that it was the sister of the girl who had been killed. Even though the reading had not been given to Jane, to her this provided undeniable proof that Loraine was connecting on a very deep level. To this day, remembering the moment she was faced with such proof gives Jane goose bumps. No one was trying to con or impress her. In fact, no one had been speaking to her at all. It was the first time in her life that she fully and truly accepted that there was life after death because she had actually known the spirit who had come through for someone else.

Since then, Jane has had readings with Loraine and reports that her own spiritual journey has brought her great joys, as well as a few sorrows. But she finds it comforting and a little exciting to know that there is a reason for everything and that someday she will go back "there."

CHAPTER 8. JACK THE RIPPER GHOST WALK
December 2011

On the evening of 12 December 2011, Loraine held a ghost walk in the White Chapel District of London in search of the spirit of the most notorious serial killer of all time, Jack the Ripper. Along with Loraine, the group included ghost detective Neil Humphries, Blue Badge tour guide Lawrence Summers, myself, a film crew led by director Laith Sami, and about 20 other people who came along to see what would happen.

FIRST STOP:

After meeting at the Whitechapel tube station, we walked to Dunward Street, the scene of the first official Jack the Ripper crime scene. Loraine began speaking right away.

"As I was walking here, I got a feeling of being pulled back, as if someone didn't want us to find out what happened that night. As you know, the murderer hasn't been found yet. I do feel that one of the girls had half her teeth missing. I feel that when he killed her it was her second encounter with him, so she already knew him. I'm getting the letter R and see her in a low-cut dress."

Loraine also went on to say that she felt the woman was a prostitute. Because of her bad teeth, she was only able to charge half a crown for her services.

Neil Humphries introduced Ripperologist and Blue Badge guide Lawrence Summers who explained that the victim found here was Mary Anne Nicholls, also called Polly Nicholls.

Loraine, Neil Humphries (ghost detective), and Lawrence Summers (Blue Badge guide and Ripper historian) at Dunward Street.

As Loraine spoke, I got a sense of an image and started to draw. It seemed particularly vivid in my mind as I drew a woman in a low-cut dress that Loraine was describing.

Sketching at Dunward Street

The image I drew at the site where
Mary Anne Nichols was found

FINDING THE BODY IN BUCKS ROW

Newspaper sketch of Mary Anne Nichols

Later I checked the historical photographs of Mary Anne Nichols. The coroner's photo shows a woman who looked like she was missing several teeth as Loraine had mentioned. The woman was found in a brown dress and was 47 at the time of her death with brown hair turning gray that she usually wore tied up or in a clip.

SECOND STOP:

We walked to the next site guided by Lawrence Summers. As we walked along, one of the women in our group shrieked.

"Someone pulled on my coat," she said. But there was no one there -- at least, no one that we could see.

We proceeded down a narrow side street to the second site. Here Loraine explained that she felt the presence of horses carrying the cart that took the body away. Loraine felt the woman who died at this spot had her eyes ripped out of their sockets and the skin of her face peeled off as well as her breasts cut off. Loraine "saw" a great deal of blood and felt the murderer put his hands up the woman and pulled her insides out. She said the killer had not even used a good sharp knife but rather a jagged one and felt he had done the same thing with at least two other victims.

Loraine felt this woman had been a busy prostitute who had nine other clients that evening before she met her end. Loraine felt she was pregnant when she died, and a little tipsy from drinking alcohol. Loraine got the distinct impression that the murderer had come to this spot many times. She sensed that he had a horse and was dropped off by other people. She felt he was interested in medicine and wanted the body to study. Loraine mentioned the name "Kitty" and wasn't sure if it was the woman's name or not as she felt the woman used two working names in addition to her real name.

Loraine sensed a strong hospital connection with the killer. It wasn't a modern hospital but had at least 20 hospital beds lined up in rows. Associated with the killer, Loraine also got a strong sense of a tall man with a name that began with the letter "R," perhaps Richard.

At this second site, I drew this sketch of a woman with dark hair in the rain. Loraine said it might have been raining but it definitely felt like a warm summer evening.

The Ripperologist Lawrence Summers then spoke and told us that this victim, named Martha Tabram, had been killed on a warm evening in August of 1888 and had been stabbed 39 times. While her breasts had not been entirely removed, she had indeed been repeatedly stabbed in the chest. According to police reports of the time, the "focus of the wounds was on the breasts, belly and groin." The coroner's photograph shows a victim with eyes closed and one side of her chest significantly deflated because of the knife wounds inflicted to that region.

According to accounts, she had last been seen by her friend Pearly Poll. The women had met two soldiers and had both gone off with them. While Martha Tabram had been murdered around the same time as the other victims and severely stabbed, Lawrence Summers explained that she was not quite as mutilated as some of

This is my sketch from the second stop where Martha Tabram was found. According to reports, she was a heavy woman with dark hair.

Discovery of the body of Martha Tabram, from <u>Famous Crimes Past and Present</u>, 1903

the other victims which left some question if she was murdered by Jack the Ripper or not.

THIRD STOP:

We proceeded to our third stop, a church yard. Lawrence Summers explained that while this was not the site of one of the murders, it is likely that the fourth official victim, Catherine Eddowes, had met her killer here and been taken around the corner where she was killed. According to Mr. Summers, in the late 1800s prostitutes felt safe in the church yard. The men could see them from beyond the fence and choose who to solicit, and the police rarely prosecuted the women in the church yard.

FOURTH STOP:

At the fourth site, Mitre Square, Loraine felt the victim had been dragged backwards while something was placed over her mouth. She felt that every piece of this victim's lower region had been ripped out and that she was the Ripper's favourite victim because he kept some of her body parts in a sort of unusual envelope. Loraine got the sense that the killer was a tall man who put his hand over the woman's face as he killed her.

At this point Loraine noted that she felt the killer was an educated man with a posh accent. She sensed he had a black and

Loraine demonstrates how the killer kept the victim from crying out.

gold badge, possibly on a carriage, that looked like a royal crest. I drew a crest with two birds, perhaps pheasants, facing each other, but am not sure if it has any meaning to the case.

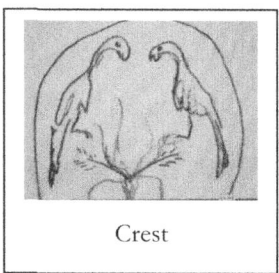

Crest

Loraine felt the killer was smug and "giggly" to have gotten away with the murders and was particularly pleased to have kept the body parts of the reproductive regions.

Lawrence Summers then explained that the woman who died at this site was Catherine Eddowes, who by all accounts was the most friendly and sociable of the victims. Her body had been mutilated severely in the most gruesome way. Her throat had been slit and her body was cut up the middle. As Loraine had surmised, this woman's womb had been cut out of her and taken away along with one kidney. There was no trace of physical intercourse and she had not been robbed.

Loraine interjected that while the killer may not have had sexual intercourse before killing the woman, she felt he was very excited by the murder and theft of the woman's organs.

Ripperologist Lawrence Summers then explained that this particular victim was killed in a very short space of time since a policeman had patrolled the area at 1:30 AM and when he returned at 1:45 AM, he found the body. There were also accounts of someone seeing a woman speaking to a man shortly after 1:30 AM. According to the timing, the killer had murdered her and taken her organs within 11 or 12 minutes. Given the speed of his assault, he may have had some kind of medical training.

The Ripperologist also mentioned that as Loraine had explained, this victim had her throat cut. This was the case with several of the victims and explains why they were not able to cry for help. Summers explained that when a throat is cut, the person might still be conscious for 20 seconds. Loraine said she felt this woman had indeed been conscious of what was happening to her as the killer cut into her.

Loraine also felt that this particular woman had a respectable funeral and that she had relatives who missed her greatly. Summers had already mentioned that this was the most sociable of the victims.

Neil Humphries added that it was around the time of this murder of Catherin Eddowes that the media frenzy took off. This was before DNA and even reliable finger-printing techniques, so it was harder to catch the killers in those days. Police investigated about four other murders of prostitutes that occurred around the same time but with the crude state of forensic science, they were not able to conclusively link them to the same killer. At the time the metropolitan police counted about 1,200 prostitutes in the area and 65 brothels, so the killer had no shortage of ladies of the night. Neil Humphries noted that when he was working as a detective in the 1990s in the Commercial Street area, the site of one of the murders, the location was still a well-known location where prostitutes looked for clients.

By this point in the evening, it had started to rain on our ghost walk. To protect the video equipment filming the event one fellow named Savik held an umbrella over the camera. As Neil spoke, the umbrella was yanked upwards and nearly wrenched out of Savik's hand. He had to grab it with both hands to keep it from going straight up into the air. There was no one above him and no wind at the time as the rain was coming straight down. He had never experienced anything like that before and found it jarring.

Listening to Loraine in Mitre Square
The umbrella protecting the video camera was inexplicably yanked upwards despite no wind.

A few moments later, a young woman in the audience named Asha felt someone stroking the front collar of her coat. As she felt it, she could see the fake fur of her collar responding, the synthetic fibres being smoothed down as the pressure moved along her coat. But no one was there! To not only feel it but to see her coat's fibres react was a disarming experience. However, in her case she didn't feel that it was a particularly angry presence but merely a curious one.

Loraine made one last comment at this site. She said she felt there was something unusual about what the killer had done to the legs of the woman killed here. As soon as she said it, I got a distinct visual image of the killer bending the legs apart and backwards just to hear her bones crack.

The historian said that the legs of this woman had been cut quite deeply and perhaps that was what Loraine was referring to, but I knew that more had been done to this poor victim. I caught up with Loraine and told her I was getting a particularly vivid image. Without explaining the image, she said, "You saw him crack her legs, too?" At that point, it got to be too much for me to "see" any more of these images. I continued on with the ghost walk, but I put away my sketch book. From that point on, I did no more drawings and experienced no more feelings or images.

FIFTH STOP:

At the fifth stop, Loraine "saw" a woman with ginger hair. She felt this wasn't the ripper's last victim but the last recorded victim. She felt the woman had been killed during a cold month and died very graphically. Lawrence Summers verified that the woman murdered at that spot died in November and was considered the Ripper's last official victim.

Loraine felt this woman was killed quickly by a tall man dressed in a black coat with nice shoes. She felt that the police did question him but let him go. Loraine also said she was getting the name George but not for the killer. She felt this was a friend.

Lawrence Summers told us the woman who died at this spot was Mary Kelly and confirmed that she had red-blonde ginger hair. At 27 she was the youngest and most attractive of all of the victims. Apparently, she wasn't normally a prostitute but needed money to pay the landlord so she had gone down Commercial Street to the 10 Bells Pub that evening to find a client and make enough money for her rent. Mr. Summers confirmed that the last person to see Mary Kelly alive was her friend George Hutchinson who had observed her talking to a well-dressed man with a cap earlier in the evening.

Loraine said that she felt the killer was after status and that he used his victims for practice. She felt he liked to cut up horses and calves and anything he could get his hands on. Loraine felt the killer had no remorse and believed the women he murdered were "not needed."

Loraine got the sense that this woman's mutilation was particularly gruesome and that the killer had removed the skin from her face and from most of her body. According to Loraine, the body was little more than a skeleton with bits of flesh and blood by the time it was found.

Lawrence Summers confirmed that this victim was the most grotesquely mutilated victim of all and was found just as Loraine described. Afterwards, I saw a police photograph that also confirmed the horrible treatment this victim had received, exactly as Loraine had explained it, with her skin and flesh cut off her body leaving little but bones. The victim had last been seen alive on the street but was found dead in her flat by her landlord's messenger boy. Apparently, the killer had gone home with her. This gave the killer a long time to mutilate the body as the murder wasn't conducted out in the open street where he could be seen.

Lawrence Summers explained that there were several suspects including John Montague Druid who killed himself around the time the murders stopped. Druid had even left a suicide note claiming to be the Ripper, but it was largely disregarded by law enforcement officials.

Loraine also felt that Druid was not the killer. She said she got a very strong sense that the killer's name was Robert, a man who sometimes went by the name Bruce and also used the alias Charles. She said he enjoyed what he did and felt no remorse. She also felt that he didn't like women and wasn't married. She got the sense that he was between 30 and 34 years old and that he wore three different hats during the killings, all of them black. She felt the "envelope" he used to store the body parts was a sort of paper bag.

Lawrence Summers confirmed that the police received body parts in the mail in a paper bag, supposedly from the killer. Loraine wasn't sure that the Ripper would give away his body parts since he loved them too much.

Loraine felt that the killer was highly educated, and the second in his class. According to her, he was displeased that he failed to be first. She sensed that he cut up the victims for anatomical knowledge and that he used two different knives. She also felt he had contracted a disease like gangrene from the body parts he kept. There was no refrigeration back then, and as the organs decayed, she feels he became infected and died shortly after his last killing. This, she feels, is why the murders stopped when they did.

As Loraine told us her final thoughts of the evening a woman standing next to me took some photographs of her. As her digital camera displayed the images, in one shot there were unusual balls of light surrounding Loraine. It wasn't dust on the lens since they only appeared on one frame. It wasn't raindrops because we were underneath a secluded overhang at that time. We showed Loraine the picture and she was not surprised. She said they were orbs representing her sprit guides, with Ramos being the strongest light, who were busy that night protecting her from harmful energy.

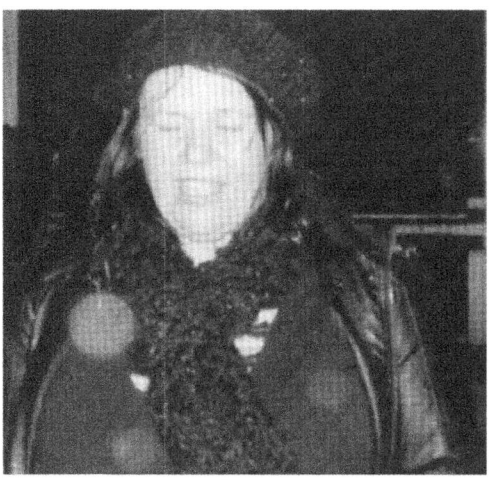

Unusual orbs of light surround Loraine. They were not raindrops; we were underneath an overhanging roof at the time.

Loraine wrapped up the evening by explaining that Jack the Ripper and his victims are tormented souls. The victims died so suddenly and tragically that their spirits have not yet come to terms with the traumatic means of their passing, which is why they are still earthbound. As for the Ripper, Loraine feels that he is afraid to face "the light" and account for what he did. Instead, she believes his spirit continues to roam the earth without a physical form. He is not allowed to pass on to a better existence until he can accept that what he did was wrong and seek forgiveness.

What was clear for me from that night is that I came away with a better understanding of what was so cruelly taken from those women back in 1888. Everyone deserves justice, and I was hoping to go back to the sites with Loraine for more clues. Some people think that such an old case couldn't possibly be solved so long after the crimes were committed. But Loraine has been instrumental in helping police solve some of the most notorious modern crimes. And with the way Loraine links in so strongly with the victims and the tormentors alike, I thought that with another encounter, she might be able to disclose more of the killer's identity.

It was a while before we were able to go back to Whitechapel for a follow-up session. But as usual when Loraine goes to work, there are always surprises in store, and her second reading with the Ripper was no exception.

CHAPTER 9. JACK THE RIPPER SECOND READING

On the 19th of July 2013, I met with Loraine at 11:00 AM at the Whitechapel train station to conduct a second reading on the Whitechapel murders. This time it was just the two of us on a summer's day with my tape recorder and no crowd of onlookers. We found a quiet corner of a pub in the area to allow her to concentrate. Below is the direct transcript from that session, with Loraine's responses shown in bold tyle.

Question: From the clues you gave before, Neil came up with a possible suspect after the first Ripper Walk. So I thought that if we came back and you get more clues and it points even more to that suspect, then maybe we can make a good case that this is the guy.

Right. Okay.

Q: Which would be great to finally catch him.

It's really funny because I've been here since ten o'clock, and as I was waking down the road, I kept getting the feeling that: "It wasn't just one of us, there were two of us."

Q: Oh, my goodness.

Yes, I kept hearing that. They kept saying "two." There were two of us. One couldn't have done all that they'd done. I asked if they were working as a team and they said, "No, we were working separately." One took advantage of what the other one was doing. What they're telling me... It's funny because obviously I've been to Canada but one of them kept showing me Canada. He had a connection with Canada. And I'm getting a sir name of "C". It's like Crem, or Cremy, Creme or something like that. I think he spent some time in Scotland. I kept seeing Scotland which is also connected with this guy. And he told me he was into medicine. I'm seeing an old-fashioned knife, like what they would cut with. Is it a scapel or scalpel? I don't know, but he was showing me one of those. So I do feel there was more than just one person that was definitely... who got the title of "The Ripper."

Q: Did one do the murders and the other one helped or did they both do the murders?

They'd both done murders but at different times. They weren't involved together, together. But as one was killing, the other took advantage of what the other was doing. So he was killing as well. So I do feel there were two serial killers. And I

do feel, though, they never knew each other but because of all the publicity, one got away with... you know he felt...

Q: Oh my goodness.

I get the feeling there was definitely two. But something to do also with, I don't know, some kind of high-up hierarchy.

Q: High up hierarchy?

Yeah. Like they were sheltered a lot. And I felt like they were sheltered by the monarchy of some sort. I feel like they were put in a bubble. It's really weird, but I kept hearing the name of Eddy. Eddy, Eddy, Eddy. I'm not sure if that was his real name, but I kept hearing Eddy, Eddy, Eddy. And there was a connection... And something Crem or Cream. But I feel there were two different people. Definitely. I do feel there were some bodies that were never found. Cut-up and disposed of. And I certainly feel there was also other stuff going on. I do feel there was more than was actually...

Q: Reported?

Reported, definitely. They tell me John had nothing to do with it, whoever John was. So they're telling me... I can see him. It's almost like... he's got a black coat or a cloak. He wasn't a bad looking man. Facial hair. And he tells me he killed Annie, whoever Annie is. He killed Annie.

Q: Is he the first one or the second one?

The first. Something to do with Bertie. Bertie. I can't tell if Bertie and Eddy are the same people. I also feel that one of these guys, and I think it's the Cremie --- it could be German, couldn't it? I'm going to say... he's also showing me that he did kill in other countries as well. So I do feel that he did... It's almost like... he's putting something on like we would say a handkerchief. Like he's putting something on a hankie and he's doing that (she gestures on the face). I'm not sure what that is, Mary, to be quite honest with you. But he's going like that (gestures rubbing over her face).

Q: He's putting the handkerchief on his face or on someone else's face?

Someone else's face. And I do feel that he shows me that he got away with murder three times in different countries. Or in a different country.

Q: That (in London) is his second one (time to murder)?

Yeah.

Q: And the first one... Now the last time (on the Ripper Ghost Walk), you said you were getting the name Richard, and then the name Robert. Robert.

Definitely, the name Robert. There was definitely a Robert. That's very prominent there. And this Robert, I do feel... I don't know whether he was made a sir, or made a something, but he was very sheltered. And something to do with an Eddy as well. I don't know if he looked after an Eddy, or had something to do with Eddy. I'm not sure. But he was a big hierarchy. They're showing me a black drawn-horse carriage. And I kept feeling it had something to do with some kind of higher monarchy stuff. Whether he worked for the monarchy, I'm not sure. But I certainly feel there was stuff there. And I'm also seeing a south London maybe connection with him. And something about books. Lots and lots of books. Something to do also with... I'm going over into Bristol or

West Country. Maybe heading towards Gloucester or Wales. That way. Bloody hell, somebody was murdered in this pub.

Q: Oh dear. From that time?

I'm not sure... no, this was a recent murder.

Q: Last time you said you were getting some sort of an old-time hospital connection.

Yes, definitely an old-time hospital. And I do feel both of these people had a connection with hospitals. Both of the Rippers... in different... I don't know. I'm not sure they worked in the same hospital. Definitely a connection in the hospitals as well.

Q: Did they work for hospitals or were they there in a hospital?

No, they did work.

Q: There was one guy whose name was Robert who was a suspect. He wasn't working at a hospital at the time but was a patient at the hospital. The police suspected him but he said how could he have done it if he was a patient. And they thought maybe he was sneaking out of the hospital and doing it.

No, that's not it. He used to rape but he didn't murder.

Q: Which one?

Robert. He raped but he didn't rape those victims. I know this is east London, but I'm definitely getting a south London link as well. I almost want to go south of the river. They're telling me there was quite a few suspects at the time but it was bad, you know. The police didn't seem to know what they were doing. But definitely two members. One of them definitely has a Canadian connection. The maple leaf is Canada, isn't it?

Q: Yes.

Yeah.

Q: So he was Canadian? Possibly Eddy?

Something to do with Eddy. He was involved with one of them. But I do feel he was more of a kind of alibi. This Eddy bloke...

Q: ...Was his alibi?

Yes, was his alibi. And definitely someone named John.

Q: Who was involved?

Yeah. But again as an alibi as well. So I do feel that there was a bit of hierarchy stuff going on. But there was definitely two. But there was definitely a Canadian, or had to do with the USA. But he tells me he killed many women. And not just over here. But he did study medicine.

Q: So he studied medicine. Killed lots of women. Possibly in Germany. Possibly in Canada. Possibly German.

I do feel there was a German connection around him because I've been hearing the name "Crem."

Q: C-R-E-A-M?

(Shakes her head). That's Cream.

Q: C-R-E-M?

Don't know. I'm just hearing "Crem."

Q: As his last name?

Yes. It's really interesting because I feel that because there were two people, that... he tells me he got away with murder, murder, murder. Not just over here but over there as well.

Q: After or before?

Before.

Q: So he did some murders overseas, possibly Canada...

Or the USA.

Q: Or the USA, and then he did some here?

(nods) He didn't do them all.

Q: And then, how did he die?

Natural causes.

Q: So he lived much longer?

He left England.

Q: Oh! He left England.

He said to me he'd done murders over there, over here. He'd done murders most of his life.

Q: Was this guy married?

His mother was very controlling. So controlling, and he hated women.

Q: So, was he married?

No. He's saying yes, but no. What's he showing me... he was forced to marry but never wanted to marry.

Q: So he doesn't consider it? Do you have a first name for him?

He's just telling me to call him Dr. Crem. Q: Dr. Crem. Spelled with a C or a K? C. Strange. Really strange. Nice looking man, actually. You'd never fail to look at him.

Q: Sideburns?

Yes.

Q: Yeah, I got that.

Nice hat on. Tall hat. I don't know whether... he specialized in gynaecology.

Q: Specialized in gynaecology?

Yeah. Abortions. He showed me lots of abortions.

Q: Abortions? And he had the royal connection possibly?

There were two doctors involved. One was a cover up.

Q: So possibly another doctor knew that he was doing this and covered it up?

Yes. He tells me it was all for science. All for medicine.

Q: So who was Robert?

He was the fellow who... I can see Robert as sure as God made little red houses. Really, really distinct. He was involved. There was more people involved.

Q: Than just the... You said he raped women.

He raped women, yes.

Q: Was he possibly involved in a cover up? Or finding the women?

He told them where to find the women. Somebody went to an asylum.

Q: One of the people who helped?

They're showing me a man... I think this would be probably the policeman who interviewed five different people. And they all had a connection.

Q: Would they... all those years ago... (The pub puts on loud music. The conversation stops, then continues.)

Definitely a connection with royalty. I was hearing the name Eddy. With the Bertie. And I do feel that one of them did rape but not murder. And I think that was the other guy...

Q: Eddy?

That was Crem. He's telling me he died, and a relatively old man, but not of natural causes. That was the other one. Crem is telling me he died with a noose around his neck.

Q: So Dr. Crem did get away with it for a while but was eventually caught?

And was hung. Yes.

Q: But not in England?

Not in England.

Q: And Eddy or Bert... died of natural causes?

Yeah.

Q: Which one was the Canadian connection?

Crem.

Q: He killed before, then here, and then he killed again after here?

Yeah.

Q: So did Eddy actually do the murders or did he just help?

He'd done some.

Q: He did some?

He'd done two. The other guy did the rest. At least three, the other one, because he removed the organs.

Q: He did what?

Crem removed their organs.

Q: Oh. So he's the one who removed the organs. What about the Robert guy?

Robert, I do feel he was just the lookout.

Q: He was just... The lookout?

He was being used. Definitely I do feel he was the scapegoat because if they got caught, they was going to pile it onto him.

Q: When you were talking to the victims, they said Robert. Could it be that he was the one who came to them?

Yes. He was the one that actually had sex with them.

Q: He enticed them, and then the other ones killed...?

The problem is that Crem didn't have sex with them. He was the one that got this Robert to get the victims. I don't know what he did with them but then he cut them up. Now I do feel the one connected with royalty did have sex with them.

Q: The one connected with royalty, Eddy or Bertie, he's the royal connection?

Yeah.

Q: And these two men didn't know each other?

Not personally.

Q: Crem or Eddy didn't now each other? So who did Robert work for?

The doctor.

Q: Could Robert have been in the hospital?

He was in the hospital, yes.

Q: As a patient?

Yes.

Q: But he was just a fall-back?

He's the one that used to go out and get the girls. And he would come in and put something on a cloth and put it on their face.

Q: Like chloroform or something? Robert did that?

Yes, because that's what the Doctor told him to do. Robert and Crem worked as a team, but the other guy, Bertie or Eddy, he worked very much alone. But he had the hierarchy around him. (Pause). Oh! That was weird. They're showing me a woman with a roundish face. Quite smart. And I believe that she was connected to a prince. To the prince? And she knew what he was doing.

Q: She knew what was going on?

Yes.

Q: So, Eddy died of natural causes as an old man, Crem was hung. What about Robert?

Something to do with Crem and a woman called Ma... Mailda... Mahilda.

Q: And she worked with Crem?

No, she was killed by him.

Q: She was killed by Dr. Crem?

(nods). Mahilda? Matilda? I don't know, something like that.

Q: And she was a smart woman?

She was very smart, and definitely murdered. But no, this one up here, the one I saw, she was in it with the prince and not Crem. But I've got them both here and they're both giving me snippets of information, so it's bloody confusing.

Q: So, there was a smart woman connected to the prince and that is different than Mahilda?

Yes. Mahilda was Crem's victim but not in England.

Q: It does sound German, doesn't it?

And the name Tom or Thomas is connected with Crem as well. And the name Florrie or Florence.

Q: Was this a victim?

No, he says. "Worse luck."

Q: Worse luck?

She wasn't his victim, worse luck. He seems very angry about this woman.

Q: You said somebody had a controlling mother.

I don't know if he was actually married to this one (Florrie) because he's showing me his wedding ring finger and he just spat on it. Nice man.

Q: (laughs) He's a nice man.

Yeah. For somebody so educated, yeah.

Q: How educated?

Medically. He liked to cut up bodies.

Q: The last time you said there was someone who was second in his class. Was that...

Crem.

Q: In medical school?

Yes, medical.

Q: Was Mahilda one of his first victims?

No.

Q: So he did a number of murders in his first country. But she knew him?

She knew him. "We both knew him," she says. He hung for her.

Q: So this was a later victim?

Yes.

Q: "We both knew him." So after he left here, he did two... at least two murders. At least where she was, because she knew his other victim. And then he hung for her, in a different country. Possibly Canada?

USA or Canada.

Q: This is pretty specific.

Yeah. Strange.

Q: Because before you were getting Thomas... I mean Robert...

Yes. Robert. He was connected with this Crem. Because Robert was... what they would say... would be the bait. To get the women.

Q: And he's the one the women would have seen?

Yes. To have sex with them. Because he liked to rape. And the doctor would come in and carve up.

Q: While they were unconscious, he would have sex with them?

Yes. He would put something over their nose.

Q: Now, if I had a last name for Robert, would you know if it was him or not, if he was the guy?

(Thinks a few moments, then laughs). Sorry, Mary. One of the last victims that was done by the man in the coach... she shows me her in her long skirt swaying and she's laughing. And it's almost like... she came around to get the money.

Q: She came around to get the money?

And she shows me him taking off his cloak and then doing what he had done.

Q: Which one?

This is the prince or the one with the royalty connection. Because I see a horse drawn carriage and letters on the side of the carriage.

Q: And this has to do with Eddy?

Definitely someone called Eddy. And Bertie. I don't know if Eddy and Bertie are connected but I kept hearing Eddy. And Bertie.

Q: So this one in the long swaying skirt, was taken in the coach?

No, he came out of the coach, paid his money, and took her back to the room. Although she was killed, she wasn't cut up.

Q: To her room?

Yes.

Q: And this is Eddy or Bertie, and he had sex and killed her? But not cut up?

Not cut up. Maybe she was strangled because I feel something around my neck.

Q: It seems like some of the victims, the earlier victims, weren't cut up as bad and the later ones were. Did Eddy/Bertie start it and the other one...

Yes. Took advantage of what was going on.

Q: So Eddy/Bertie did a couple (of the murders)? Maybe two?

Yeah.

Q: And then the other one did at least three... here, and them some more somewhere else, and possibly some before?

Yeah.

(The conversation veers off-topic for a while, then resumes.)

Going back to the Jack the Ripper, it was a lot more complicated than people think it was. There were a lot of twists and turns, and definitely more than two people involved. Because I've got three people being involved at the moment and at different levels, do you understand?

Q: Yeah.

And I do feel that the Eddy/Bertie one had a lot of cover-up. A lot of people knew what he was up to. I do feel a lot of stuff was going on. And I do feel that a lot of the Bertie cover up had to do with the hierarchy.

Q: And then the other one had Thomas to come in to set up the crimes and then he would finish it off?

No.

Q: Not Thomas, I mean Robert. Sorry.

Robert. Would there be a D name connected with this Robert?

Q: Yes. As a last name?

A "D" name.

Q: Yes.

So he had his fingers in a lot of business, this Robert. He would do anything, absolutely anything, to get a bit of money. I don't think he was scared to venture into anything for money.

Q: This kind of makes sense, because they've never been able to find the one person. They talked to some of these guys and they were able to get out of it somehow. And if there was more than one...

Definitely more than one.

Q: They would have an alibi for some.

Definitely an alibi. What's an abattoir?

Q: It's a slaughter house. A French word for slaughter house. Who is this connected with?

This is to do with Crem. He says it was like an abattoir. "So easy, so easy. Me and Robert were so much a team." Hmm. There you go.

Q: Wow.

So, three people that we know of.

Q: So Bertie was connected to the prince or Bertie was the prince?

Connected. There was one of the victims attacked just down the road.

Q: So, Eddy did the first couple (of murders) and then the other guy, Crem...

...Did the more vicious attacks. Somebody's body was found in this alleyway. Although I don't think it was connected to this case.

Q: You can imagine all kinds of things could go on here.

I definitely feel someone was stabbed right here in this pub.

Q: Recently?

Within that last 30 years.

Do you want to ask (the bar-tender?)

(The conversation moves off the Ripper topic).

----------End of Transcript ----------------------------

Apparently, the identity of Jack the Ripper may be more convoluted than previously believed. The five generally accepted (canonical) victims of Jack the Ripper were attacked from August 1888 through November 1888. These include Mary Ann Nichols (August 1888), Annie Chapman (September 1888), Elizabeth Stride

(September 1888), Catherine Eddowes (September 1888) and Mary Jane Kelly (November, 1888). In addition, from February of 1888 to February of 1891, there were 11 additional women assaulted in London who have been considered possible victims of Jack the Ripper. Three of the earlier victims initially survived but died shortly thereafter. Two of the later bodies were so mutilated that identification could not be ascertained. After the London murders, one possible Ripper victim, Carie Brown, was found murdered in Manhattan, New York in April of 1891 with stab wounds similar to those inflicted in London. Several suspects have been proposed as possible candidates for the murders, including three people who fit the descriptions from Loraine's second reading on the topic. The information from this second reading, for the most part, does not conflict with her original reading from the ghost walk in December 2011 but further explains various aspects, separating the pieces of information she came up with then into three distinctly different people.

There indeed was an "Eddy" connected with royalty who has been previously proposed as a possible suspect. This was Prince Albert Victor, known as "Eddy" to his friends, who was the son of Prince Albert Edward (Victoria's oldest son known as Bertie and who eventually became King Edward VII). According to sources, Prince Albert Victor was of limited intelligence. He died in 1892 of influenza, although there were unconfirmed rumours it was syphilis. Eddy apparently had alibis for all five of the canonical victims. However, four women were attacked before the first of the canonical victims. Could Prince Albert Victor have indeed started the spree of lethal attacks on women, perhaps in a sex-gone-wrong scenario, which was later taken up by someone else? If so, could Eddy's father Bertie have known about his son's participation and been aware of a cover-up? For more on the Ripper suspects and victims, considerable information is available at www.casebook.org which provides references and evidence both for and against the various theories that have been proposed over the years.

Regarding Loraine's "Dr. Crem," there was indeed a Dr. Thomas Neill Cream who has been considered a suspect. Born in

Dr. Thomas Neill Cream

1850 in Scotland where the pronunciation of his name might well have sounded like "Crem," he moved with his family to Canada as a child and attended McGill University as a medical student. After meeting Flora Elizabeth Brooks who became pregnant with his child, Cream performed an abortion on her that nearly killed her, and was forced by his father to marry her. The next day (11th September 1876), he escaped the marriage by leaving Canada for England. There he enrolled as a graduate student at London's St. Thomas's Hospital in London which was south of the River Thames opposite the Houses of Parliament.

Cream returned to Canada a few years later and became an abortionist, an illegal profession at the time. He was suspected in the murder of Kate Gardener who was found near his office beside a bottle of chloroform. He was arrested but released. Cream moved to the USA and was suspected in the murder of Julia Faulkner. Again, he was released.

He was eventually convicted of another murder in the Chicago area when he poisoned a man who accused him of having an affair with his wife. Cream was convicted and jailed at the Illinois State Penitentiary at Joliet in 1881. He received a life sentence for his crime although prison records claim he was released in July of 1891. He was gifted an inheritance of $16,000 and after collecting it in Canada, he again travelled to England. However, by the time he arrived, his fortune seems to have disappeared, forcing him to live in humble conditions in the Lambeth area of South London.

When two local women, Matilda Clover and Ellen Donworth, died of poisoning, Cream was questioned but released. He was implicated in two more murders but escaped conviction. Desperate for funds, he blackmailed another man for the murders, providing remarkable details. However, his extortion attempt backfired and he was eventually charged and found guilty of the death of Matilda Clover and he was sentenced to hang.

On the 15th of November 1892, according to the hangman James Billington, Cream's last words on the gallows were "I am Jack..." However, he died before completing the sentence. Was this a confession attempt for the Ripper murders? Theorists have noted that Dr. Cream's handwriting shows a similarity to the handwriting of two of the Ripper letters. As a suspect, though, Dr. Cream has been considered problematic. His preferred method of murder was poison, particularly strychnine, which does not seem to have been used in the Ripper murders. But if Cream was working in tandem with an accomplice on the Ripper murders, it could explain a change in method.

The biggest problem with Cream as a suspect is his jail service in Illinois at the time of the Whitechapel murders. However, some theorists have noted that early in his criminal career, Cream plead innocent to a crime of bigamy, claiming it was someone else with his name and description on the grounds that he was in jail at the time. The authorities confirmed that such a "look-alike" man was incarcerated at that time. His lawyer, Marshall Hall, presented such a strong case that Cream had a double in the criminal world that Dr. Cream was released from the bigamy charges. Apparently, Marshall Hall was convinced that Cream and his double went by the same name and used each other's terms of imprisonment as alibis for each other.

It is of note that the prisons in the Chicago area in the late 1800s were well known for corruption. Could an educated, well-travelled man like Cream, clever enough to evade numerous murder charges, have successfully bribed jail officials? It is certainly possible given his early release from jail and the disappearance of his $16,000 inheritance, a veritable fortune at the time. If his inheritance had been used to bribe prison officials or pay for a double, perhaps his premature release from his sentence at Joliet "for good behaviour" may have actually happened earlier than the official records indicate.

The third man mentioned in Loraine's updated reading, Robert with a "D," may well have been Ripper suspect Robert

Robert D'Onston Stephenson
1841- 1916

D'Onston Stephenson. Born near Hull in 1841, Robert D'Onston Stephenson studied chemistry in Munich and medicine in Paris. He served the crown as a custom's officer in Hull but left in disgrace before arriving in London. A man with burdensome gambling debts, he once served a stint as an army surgeon. He checked into the London Hospital in Whitechapel in July of 1888 for a rest cure from back pain and remained there until December of 1888. Thus, he would have been in the area at the time so many of the murders took place.

Theorists have suggested that based on Robert D'onston Stephenson's writings, much of which focused on obsessive details of the Ripper cases, he may have been motivated by black magic, another favourite topic of his. Perhaps, though, as a possible accomplice, simpler motivation might have sufficed -- money, or the influence of a charismatic lead killer.

The information Loraine came up with in this second Ripper reading corresponds to these three suspects with such clarity that readers might wonder if Loraine looked up Jack the Ripper information before the session. It would certainly have been possible. But as Loraine's biographer, granted unlimited access to her work from all angles, I know that this is not how Loraine operates. She routinely gives readings of similar specificity to people she has never met. At her shows and personal readings, she doesn't collect prior personal information. No credit card names or personal details are required in advance that could be used to look up an individual's history. She has no staff or assistants working for her who could research the many people she reads each year, nor could they through her practice of cash box 'at-the-door.' Between her children, grandchildren, the steady stream of word-of-mouth clients, and the barrage of messages she receives from the other side, she often says with a hearty laugh, "When would I possibly have the time?"

As I have observed over and over, Loraine's process is very simple; she listens. No need for tricks, she listens to her inner hearing. For her, it's as easy as listening to the radio or the telephone, but actually simpler because there's no device involved; the "voices" come to her.

Sometimes with more than one "voice" conveying information at the same time, it can get confusing. Of the 10 - 20 percent of the time that Loraine is wrong on a reading, sometimes the message is off by a twist. It might be the right message but for a different person. At the second Ripper reading, Loraine said that "Dr. Crem" was hung but not in England. Actually, Dr. Thomas Neill Cream was, in fact, hung in London outside Newgate Prison in 1892. This was after the Ripper murders had ceased and Cream was caught in England after engaging in

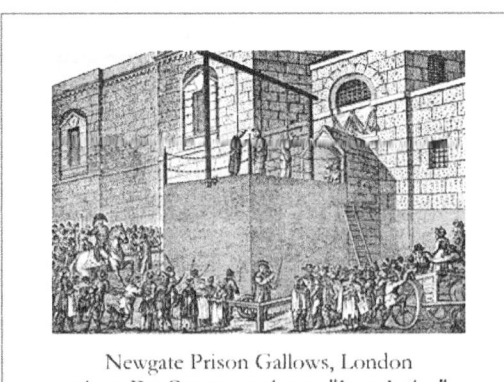

Newgate Prison Gallows, London
where Dr. Cream was hung. "I am Jack..."

what would become his final killing spree.

The idea that there may not have been a solitary Jack the Ripper is an intriguing one, and might well explain why a single generally accepted candidate has not emerged despite considerable effort spent to fine one. While many single suspects have been theorized, none have yet been proven.

DNA "EVIDENCE?"

In September of 2014, there was a claim by an author that a single suspect had emerged, a Polish Jewish immigrant named Aaron Kosminski. According to this theory, a shawl taken from the crime scene in 1888 by Acting Sergeant Amos Simpson was later auctioned in 2007, purchased, and found to contain DNA of both the victim Catherine Eddowes and suspect Aaron Kosminski. However, at the time of the author's sensational claim and the release of his book, no substantiation, verification, or scientific/forensic review of the DNA evidence was performed.

According to Sir Alec Jeffreys who invented the DNA forensic technique, this theory is "an interesting but remarkable claim that needs to be subjected to peer review with detailed analysis of the provenance of the shawl and the nature of the claimed DNA match with the perpetrator's descendants and its power of discrimination; no actual evidence has yet been provided." (The Independent News, www.Independent.co.uk, 07 Sept. 2014). In addition to the lack of DNA verification through a technical review, the questionable provenance of the shawl and its potential for cross-contamination over the hundred-plus years of being handled by any number of people, there are additional significant problems with this theory.

According to Neil Humphries, former Detective with Scotland Yard who has examined what has been obtained from the police records, all persons who visited the Catherine Eddowes murder scene were recorded at the time and their names supplied to the coroner. Yet there is no mention or documentation of Amos Simpson having visited the crime scene. The body of Katherine Eddowes in Mitre Square was found by PC Watkins of the City of London Police. The murderer made good his escape into Goulston Street where he left the only clue, a bloodied apron that the police believed was used to wipe the murder weapon. This was found by a PC Alfred Long and not Simpson. Given that Catherine Eddowes was murdered on the same night as Elizabeth Stride, a night the police missed the Ripper by a matter of minutes as they converged on Mitre Square, it would have been difficult for Simpson to access the crime scene and remove evidence without being seen by other officers.

Other problems with Aaron Kominski as a suspect remain. He did not come to police notice until two years after the Ripper murders had ceased. At this time, he was institutionalized -- not for violence but for "self-mutilation," which was polite parlance for masturbation. Consigned to living in an asylum for the rest of his life, he was not considered particularly violent as his only known acts of aggression included throwing a chair at an asylum worker and once threatening his sister with a knife. No doubt Aaron Kominski was considered by many to be an unsavory character as he was a vagrant who refused to bathe which gave him a foul smell.

Eventually he was regarded by Assistant Commissioner Macnaughten and Deputy Assistant Commissioner Anderson to be a prime Ripper suspect. However, other senior investigators at the time did not agree. They questioned how such an odorous man who spoke only Yiddish could entice women into dark alleyways. Investigators who questioned Aaron Kominski's culpability included the City of London Commissioner Henry Smith who headed the murder investigation of Catherine Eddowes in Mitre Square, and the highly respected Detective Inspector Edmund Reid from Leman Street Police who investigated the murders not from his desk but on the street in the areas where they occurred.

If a formal peer review were to be conducted which did confirm the DNA on the shawl and could rule out degradation and possible cross contamination, it still would not prove murder but only contact. Given Catherine Eddowes' profession, contact with a variety of clients and men would be expected.

More than any other theory, to me the multiple murderer scenario based on Loraine's channelling of the spirit world makes a great deal of sense. According to Neil Humphries, there is no known obvious link connecting Dr. Thomas Cream, Robert D'onston Stephenson, and Albert Victor. However, all three remain possible suspects until they can be irrefutably eliminated. No doubt, Ripperologists will continue to hotly debate the pros and cons of their preferred suspects for years to come. Perhaps that is only right, not so much for the arguments over the case specifics but to ensure remembrance of those women and what was taken from them.

In the meantime, I will leave Loraine's readings on the subject documented here, recorded for readers to consider as they choose. As for me, I appreciate the overall message Loraine's readings serve to convey -- that there is no escaping the consequences of one's actions, whether in this world or the next.

CHAPTER 10. AN ANGRY MOTHER

Of all the troubled spirits Loraine has dealt with, there was one that intrigued me above all the rest. This was a spirit who Loraine had "met" at a Mind Body Soul demonstration at Kempton Park in 2009. In the audience that day was a woman named Kathy. Loraine sensed the spirit of Kathy's departed mother around her. As Loraine gave Kathy a reading in the packed audience, this spirit manifested its presence quite forcefully. According to the people who were there that day, the sky went from clear blue to dark and stormy, the doors rattled, and the windows shook. I wasn't there to see it but had heard about it from a few different people.

Over the next several months, Kathy had a few private readings with Loraine, and Kathy's angry mother would always come through. Sometimes her mother's spirit seemed to soften slightly, but then it would come back at the next reading just as hostile as before.

I was intrigued. What, I wondered, had happened to this woman to make her soul so outraged?

Later I had my own encounter with this angry soul. It was during Loraine's Uxbridge show on 3 March 2011, one of the first of Loraine shows I attended as a psychic sketch artist.

During the show in Uxbridge that night, one of the people in the audience was a woman named Susan. I drew Susan and a spirit image above her of a very bossy woman, a spirit who was determined not to let death stop her from getting the last word.

Loraine said to Susan, "Your mother is here. She's a really strong energy. And your sister is here, too, right in this room. But your sister isn't dead. She's sitting right there, two rows away."

"No," said Susan. "I came alone tonight. That's not my sister."

"Yes, she is," said Loraine. "Your mother's spirit is telling me that you're trying to trick me, to see if what I'm telling you is real. Well, I have to say, your mother is really here, and she says: *Don't fecking lie to the psychic.*"

This was clearly a spirit with an irate edge.

Susan denied it again but after Loraine's persistence, Susan reluctantly confessed that her sister was indeed sitting where

Loraine indicated, and that she was just trying to make sure that Loraine was a real psychic.

The reading continued, and Loraine told the sisters that their mother was still angry and had a lot of unresolved issues. They agreed. Kathy told me later that when her mother had come through so dramatically at the Kempton show, at the same moment, her sister Susan, who had stayed home, had called her with strange news.

"Has anything odd just happened to you?" Susan had asked. "Because my light bulb just exploded, and it was really bizarre."

Exploding light bulbs were just one of the many ways their mother has manifested her energy since her crossing. That night after the show, Kathy told me of ash trays that have gone flying across the room and cupboards that have opened and slammed shut all by themselves.

Following is the picture I drew of Kathy, Susan, and their mother's spirit that night in Uxbridge.

KATHY, SUSAN, AND THEIR MOTHER still trying to get the last word.
Afterwards, Kathy told me her mother sometimes wore her hair in that style.

Seven months later, in October 2011, Loraine returned to Uxbridge to do a second show. Once again Kathy and Susan attended. About halfway through the session, Loraine went up to Susan and Kathy.

"Have you lost your mum?" Loraine asked. Susan agreed. Having read Susan and Kathy before, of course Loraine had already been exposed to the loss of their mother. But that doesn't explain how with each successive reading, Loraine comes up with more facts and specifics that weren't previously discussed.

Loraine said, "She's telling me that she's much calmer."

Susan said she didn't believe that.

Loraine asked Kathy if she was a light sleeper. When Kathy agreed, Loraine told her that it was her mother's spirit that continues to wake her up because her mother is trying to get her attention.

Loraine said, "She did love you, although I believe she loved you in her own way. I feel she was a little messed up in the head."

The sisters later revealed that their mother suffered brain damage before she died.

Loraine said that there were terrible things in their mother's childhood, and that she had been badly abused with both physical and mental abuse, and that there was a story to be told about what their mother had been through.

Then Loraine said that their mother did love arguing and making an impact. Even her funeral made an impact, Loraine insisted, and said that all hell broke loose at their mother's funeral. The sisters agree that it did.

Loraine said that their mother used strong words. "Everything was "f" this and "f" that, and now she tells me: *I fecking hated my family. I fecking hated them all, really*." The sisters roll their eyes. Apparently, they had heard the same things from their mother when she was alive.

Loraine continued. "She tells me she is sorry for all the pain she caused you, although she says you probably won't believe her about that."

A little too vehemently, Susan said, "No, I don't."

Loraine asks, "Who is Mary?"

"That was our mum's name," Kathy explained.

Loraine said, "She's also telling me there was a baby that was left for dead, after it was born. Do you understand? She's giving me two babies, here. I don't know if they were stillborn..."

Kathy confirmed that her mother had two babies that didn't survive.

Loraine said, "She feels that nobody knew the real truth about her. They just couldn't be bothered. I do feel your mother couldn't show her love because she never was given love herself."

Kathy confirmed that this was very likely.

Loraine said that Mary seemed like a very hard cookie to crack, and that her daughters never really knew a lot of things about her.

The daughters agreed.

Loraine ended their reading by saying that there was still a lot of violence in Mary's spirit. Again, her daughters couldn't help but agree with that.

As I sketched the energy I felt, I realized that this was my second sketch of Mary, the angry mother with the troubled soul. I also noticed that I was drawing her hair with a lot more curly waves this time. I wondered about this since the daughters sitting in front of me had fairly straight hair.

I showed Kathy the sketch and asked her why I might be drawing her mother's hair so curly this time.

"My Mum's hair was curly," she said. "My sister and I have curly hair, too, but we straighten ours."

KATHY, SUSAN, and my second drawing of their mother's energy, confused this time more than angry

Despite the reading and the obvious sense of anger expressed, I got the feeling that Mary's spirit was wound up with confusion and frustration. It seemed to me that she had spent so much of her life in anger that now that she was in the spirit world, it was the only way she could relate. I also felt that her spirit would like to somehow get rid of her negative energy. I had no idea if that was even possible, or how you could go about trying to do such a thing.

After the first book came out, Loraine told me that I would eventually do more books on her -- perhaps a whole series. At the time, I couldn't imagine what else I could possibly say about Loraine's work. The first book portrayed such extraordinary events that I couldn't imagine what else I could possibly write.

But as Loraine began her ghost walks and the various troubled souls revealed themselves, the theme for this second book took shape.

There are several reasons why a spirit might not permanently move onto a higher plane. They might wish to return on occasion to visit loved ones. Or they might have had a sudden death and become confused, unable to accept or understand their fate.

According to Loraine, there are damaged spirits that are afraid to move on because they did terrible things while alive, and fear what will happen to them if they go onto a higher spiritual plane and have to face what they did.

However, based on what Loraine has been shown on the other side, even damaged souls can be redeemed if they can grow enough to seek forgiveness. Unfortunately, not all souls are capable of such growth, and without it, they cannot be redeemed. Unable to move on, the physical world is haunted by spirits who are trapped here. They can't move onto the next spiritual plane, but without substance, they're no longer able to fully exist in the physical world, either. Fortunately, while they might be able to cause mischief with energy fluctuations, they are not able to do any real damage in the physical world. According to Loraine, it is simply not permitted.

Some of the spirits Loraine encountered on the ghost walks were victims. Others like Matthew Hopkins, John Stearne, and the Ripper were the perpetrators whose lack of repentance trapped their souls between this world and the next.

But what about Kathy's mother, Mary? This was a soul who claimed to have experienced terrible things during her life, a spirit determined to manifest her continued presence, and who sent messages with equal measures of apologies as well as insults.

Could such a spirit be redeemed? I thought it was worth a try to find out.

I asked Loraine if she would be willing to do a long reading for Kathy, to give her mother's spirit the time to get her full story out. I agreed to be on hand to document whatever happened and record Mary's story.

Loraine thought this was a good idea. Kathy was nervous but said that if there was any chance it might give her mother's spirit some peace, then she was willing to try. Kathy knew little of her mother's youth, except that her mother frequently said that her life had been so difficult that people would find it hard to believe. Kathy felt that by giving her mother the chance to get her story out, perhaps she might at last be able to let go of her anger and embrace peace.

Loraine and I agreed to meet Kathy at her house on 30 November 2011. I know that Kathy and I were both nervous as the date approached. After all, this was an angry and active spirit. Was it really a good idea to encourage such a soul to express herself?

Two days before the reading, one of the lights in my house started to act in an odd manner. It would flicker violently, sending strobe-like shadows dancing across the room. But as soon as it caught my attention and I looked up at the bulb, it would immediately revert to normal -- no problems with the light bulb at all. This happened again and again, at least a dozen times. After a while, I avoided going into that particular room or even looking in there. It just seemed creepy, as if something was manipulating the light bulb to get my attention -- something that in a purely physical world shouldn't exist. I also had the feeling that the timing of the odd flickering light with Kathy's upcoming reading was no coincidence.

Finally, it was the day of the reading. Loraine and I planned to drive separately to Uxbridge and have the reading at Kathy's house. However, that morning, Loraine's car wouldn't start. She phoned from West Sussex to say she couldn't get out of the driveway and asked me if I could drive up to Uxbridge and get Kathy and bring her back with me. I agreed.

That day, 30 Nov 2011, I was caught in some of the worst traffic I have ever experienced. It took over two and a half hours to drive to Uxbridge to collect Kathy, and another and two and a half hours to drive to Loraine's town, a distance that was only 45 miles away. No matter what alternate route we took, we found that the traffic converged on us there as well. Of course I've been stuck in traffic before, but on that day, I felt as if wherever I drove became the new epicentre of England's worst traffic. As the hours ticked away and our progress continued at a snail's pace, we heard from Loraine that her car was working perfectly again; there was nothing wrong with it. She couldn't explain why it had refused to start earlier, but as we were already on the way, there was nothing she could do but wait for us to arrive.

After nearly five hours of driving a distance that should have taken 90 minutes, we neared Loraine's town. As we did, the sun disappeared behind a cloud. Despite the sunny forecast, the sky turned gray and rain poured down on my car. By this point, the entire mood of the day had been so strange that I was no longer surprised. Part of me wondered if someone or something was trying to impede this meeting and prevent us from finding out the truth about Kathy's mother.

I turned to Kathy and told her about the odd way my light had flickered at home.

She said, "Then when you look at it, it turns normal again, right?" I asked how she knew. Apparently, this is something that started happening at Kathy's house shortly after her mother died. Kathy feels it is her mother's special "code" for getting her attention and showing when her spirit is around. I couldn't argue with that.

Finally, Kathy and I arrived at Loraine's house. Loraine prepared a quick meal to recharge us all. Loraine said she had also felt there were some unusual impediments to the reading as if some force was trying to prevent it from happening.

Kathy was anxious and I was wondering if maybe this wasn't such a good idea. But Loraine was calm. After all, this was not some thoughtless party game. Instead, Loraine is a woman who has spent her entire life communicating with energies beyond the physical plane. Advised by her spirit guides, she has made this her life's work. Loraine implicitly trusts that her spirit guides will protect her and she trusts the process. Her gentle but unshakeable confidence reassured Kathy and me, and we all sat down to begin the reading. I wasn't sure what messages Loraine would receive but I thought that by this point in the very strange day, I was beyond being shocked by whatever would come out.

I was wrong.

Recreated from my tapes and notes, here is an account of the session. Where Loraine directly channelled the voice of Kathy's mother's spirit, I have used italics.

* * *

Loraine gets comfortable on the couch while Kathy sits on a love seat to her right. I sit on a footstool facing them both, my notebook in hand. I turn on the tape recorder and reiterate that the purpose of the reading is to give the troubled spirit of Kathy's mother the chance to get her story out so that she can put her anger behind her. It takes Loraine no time at all to connect and start to speak.

"Your mother is here," Loraine tells Kathy. "And your grandmother as well. Your Nan (grandmother) is coming forward as a sort of peacemaker. Your mother tells me that she was quite fussy about her hair. She always wanted her hair to be just so, and she's putting on gloss lipstick, too."

Kathy agrees; these were her mother's habits.

"Now there are a lot of things that she took to the grave," Loraine explains. "She's introducing me to four babies that never made it, and she feels really guilty about two of them. One baby was just before you, and one was just after you."

Kathy knew there were other siblings who didn't survive their birth.

"Life was hard," Loraine continues. "And she tells me she doesn't want to scream and shout anymore."

"I'm not so sure about that," says Kathy.

"She's telling me she's got a story to be told," says Loraine. "But now she's telling me that she hates your sister, Susan. She wants to know why Susan didn't come today."

Kathy doesn't seem too surprised.

"She's showing me some bread," Loraine says, "with nothing on it but butter. Do you understand that?"

"Bread and butter was her favourite," Kathy explains.

"She's giving me the name Mary."

"That was her name," Kathy tells us.

"And also the name Bridie, or Bridget."

Kathy explains that was one of her mother's cousins.

"And Joe," Loraine continues. "Who's Joseph?"

"That was the second name of my Granddad."

"Not your Granddad, this is a different Joe. He was her first love, before she met your dad."

This is an area of her mother's life that Kathy can't confirm or deny.

Loraine explains that Mary is not displaying much affection for her husband and that she really hated her life. People saw her as confident and bubbly, but she was miserable. She swore a lot and really missed Ireland.

Kathy confirms all of those things. Her mother used curse words liberally. She had come from Ireland as a child and always talked about it.

Loraine continues. "She says all she wanted to do was to go back to Ireland and die. She's quite bitter and says there was a lot she wanted to achieve in life that she didn't because of the bloody kids. She says that when she was young her family was very religious. Who was David or Danny?"

Kathy explains that her mother had a childhood friend named Danny.

"She's telling me that she didn't want to be where she was in life, especially towards the end. She says she had a lot of sexual abuse in her life. She says that as a kid, she was interfered with by a string of men. It started when she was four or five. She shows me a connection with the Polish War Memorial."

"Her brother-in-law was Polish."

Loraine shivers a moment before going on. "She tells me everyone hated her. That she was made to feel like a liar and a reject when she was only seven years old. She tells me it was a man down the road who started abusing her, a man named McMann. He acted like he was holier than God but secretly he was interfering with all the kids. Now, who is Tom?"

"He was her husband," says Kathy.

"She doesn't have a good thing to say about him. She says, *What a fecking thing he was, what a fecking thing he turned out to be.* I've asked her why she has to keep swearing."

Kathy laughs. "It wouldn't be her if she didn't swear."

"At least she doesn't use the C word," Loraine says. "She uses 'bastard' and everything else, but not the C word."

"No," Kathy confirms. "Everything but the C word."

"She tells me that men let her down. Were you with her when she got rid of one of her babies?"

"No," says Kathy.

"She's telling me that one of her kids watched her when she got rid of one of the babies."

This surprises Kathy.

"Yes," Loraine tells us. "She did it herself. She gave herself an abortion, and she nearly bled to death. She made herself get drunk then she put a crochet hook up herself. Twice she did that."

Kathy shakes her head. "Bloody hell."

"She says it was really painful, but she didn't feel she had a choice. She didn't have anything. She didn't even know who the dad was. Who's Annie? Annie who was four doors away?"

"That was when I was really young," Kathy explains. "I didn't remember anything about my mother's neighbours."

"She says that Annie helped her, but that her parents hated her. She says that nobody loved her. She tells me that her kids hated her as well and didn't think she was up to being a mother."

"That was her perception," says Kathy. "But it isn't true."

"She says that towards the end she was a little bit, well, deranged."

Kathy agrees with that.

"She's showing me that she pulled someone's hair. Whose hair did she pull?"

"She did that with me and my sister."

"She yanked it really hard," Loraine says. "I'm also seeing Swan Vesta matches."

Kathy explains that those were the matches her mother always used.

"One of the kids put a match to paper and almost burned the house down."

Kathy confesses, "That was me."

"Was it?" Loraine seems surprised. "She says she never knew which one of you girls did it. Until now."

Kathy laughs to have been caught. Of all the things she anticipated might come out of this reading, she hadn't expected that.

"Who's the alcoholic?" Loraine asks.

Kathy tells us it was her mother's sister.

Loraine says that this woman has crossed over as well, and Kathy confirms that her aunt is dead. Loraine explains that Mary's sister was also abused as a child. When they were children back in Ireland, there were three priests involved. Their uncles were also in on it as well. There were nine of them who abused her. It was like a paedophile ring.

Kathy confirms there were nine men her mother would have seen as uncles.

"A woman abused her as well," Loraine explains. "Who was Margaret?"

Kathy says, "That was my mother's aunt."

Loraine stops a moment as if listening to an inner voice. Then she says, "Margaret didn't abuse her sexually. But she would hit Mary if she didn't sleep with John."

"John was Margaret's husband."

Loraine continues. "She tells me that John was really rough with them. She's going on about Jerry and tells me that when she was 14 she was pregnant with Jerry. Or Terry. He was one of the uncles."

"Yes, she had an uncle Terry."

"She tells me that her own mother didn't know."

"That's right, my grandmother didn't have a clue."

"She feels that her mother was a bit thick to be so unaware of all these things that happened right under her nose. She says: *Nobody believed us kids*, and it went on for so long that your mother hated sex at the end. She hated even touching other people. She wouldn't even give her own kids a cuddle. She says she fecking hated anything like that."

"That's true."

"She tells me that she used to say, 'Have your dinner and shut up.' "

"Exactly. That's the way my mother told us she loved us."

It is clear that this is an unusual set of family dynamics, and I have to admire Kathy's calm acceptance of her mother's failings.

Loraine continues. "She did make sure that neither of her children was touched. She would have gone crazy if that had happened, even though she says she hates your bleeding sister."

Loraine herself seems surprised at the difference between the words of protection one minute juxtaposed against words of hate the next.

"That's just the way she was," Kathy explains. "She always had to say she hated one of us. Today, it's my sister. Tomorrow, it could be me. So I've learned not to take any of that personally."

The acceptance that Kathy calmly displays speaks volumes.

"Who went to prison?" Loraine asks. "And who is Sheila? And Elizabeth. Kitty. And Norah."

Kathy explains that her aunt Elizabeth often was jailed for drunk and disorderly conduct. Kitty was her grandmother's friend, but she doesn't know about the others.

"She's telling me when she was young, she had to stand there while all the men lined up to touch her. She was only nine at the time."

"That must have been when they still lived in Ireland," says Kathy.

Loraine agrees.

Kathy is confused. "Then why did my mother want to go back to Ireland so badly?"

"Because she needed to make peace with the country," says Loraine. "It wasn't Ireland's fault, it was just those people who did it. She says she was warned not to tell her mother what was going on or she would have been killed. It was your grandfather who started it. He was the first one to sexually abuse your mother, his own daughter. Then he charged the other men money and they all took their turns. These men came from the pubs while your grandmother was out doing her cleaning jobs. That's when they would touch the children."

Kathy nods. "That's right, my grandmother used to be a cleaner."

"Your aunt is here and says that's why she became an alcoholic."

"She certainly did," Kathy says. "In the 1960s, she was well up there. She went to wild parties with Jimi Hendrix and Mick Jagger. I think she had them both."

Loraine confirms. "For a while, she was a prostitute. But with all the men she had as an adult, even more men were forced on her as a child. About 30 men by the age of ten. And their father got a penny for each one. This was his beer and fag money -- none of it ever went to buy shoes for the kids. He used to say, 'Come on, Mary. Take your knickers off and do what you do best.' "

This is hard news for Kathy to hear. She thinks about it a moment and asks, "Did her own father get her pregnant? Was my grandfather actually my father?"

Loraine is quiet a moment. Then she says, "We've hit a raw nerve there, because she's gone and clammed up on me."

"I hope it's not true," says Kathy.

Loraine asks the question out loud. "Is Kathy's grandfather also her father?" She waits for an answer to come to her. Then Loraine says, "No, your grandfather is not your father. Your real father is your Uncle Ben."

Kathy thinks about this a moment. Then she says, "No, I don't believe it. I look too much like my father's side of the family to have come from Uncle Ben. My mother is just saying that to wind me up."

"Yeah," Loraine agrees, "but the truth is that your Uncle Ben used to do it to her as well, but he wasn't that bloody clever. He couldn't usually finish the job."

This isn't very comforting to Kathy.

"*It's all right for you,*" Loraine insists. "*You can say your mind. But we weren't allowed. We had to be seen and not heard.*"

Kathy nods. "That was my grandfather's saying."

"*Sit in the corner and eat a bit of bread, and that was our lot.*" Loraine continues. "*Father Cyril used to bring us sweets. Then he would tell us to go to church and pray for our sins, the sins that he created. There was a long staircase at church where the sex went on. The priests used to call us down after Sunday mass to wait for them. All the other kids thought we were special. They didn't know what was going on. Your grandfather charged the priests, too. They gave him seven guineas, 40 fags, and a penny for each time.*"

Meanwhile, your poor grandmother barely had enough to feed everyone. Now your mother's showing me when she came to England. She says she left a trail of mystery behind her. She used to have flashbacks of those times that she had been forced to go with all of those men."

Kathy says, "I'm surprised that despite all of this, she always talked about going back to Ireland."

Loraine nods. "She wanted to kill them. Every fecking one of them. She says they killed her sister."

"My aunt? No, she drowned."

"She did it herself," Loraine says. "She couldn't live with what was done to her and she killed herself. They abused her, just the way they abused Mary, then Elizabeth, then her."

"That makes sense," says Kathy, "and solves the mystery of how my aunt could have drowned the way she did. We just thought she was a drunk and a druggie."

"She was," Loraine explains. "But it was her father that made her that way."

I am getting confused keeping all the sisters and aunts straight so I ask Kathy, "Which aunt was this?"

Kathy looks at Loraine and says, "Ask my mother. She'll tell you."

Loraine thinks a moment, then she says: "*Delores.*"

Kathy shakes her head. "Delores was her nickname. Her real name was Dot."

"*You've got that backwards,*" Loraine tells her. "*Her real name was Delores.*"

I ask Loraine, "Has Mary met up on the other side with her sister Delores?"

Loraine says that she has, but she's not happy about it. She says Mary's not happy to be with anyone because she doesn't need anyone.

Kathy finds this amusing. "She's FOUND her sister and is WITH her but she doesn't NEED her?"

"Yep," Loraine snaps, then she sighs. "She says this is getting rather boring."

We all laugh at that. After all we have gone through to allow Mary's spirit to get her story out, this rare chance to set the record straight *from beyond the grave*, she has the nerve to complain that we're not exciting enough? It is a strange kind of humour, but it strikes us all as very funny, and it's a relief that something has broken the tension.

Kathy says, "That's her all right. She always was a petulant cow."

Loraine says, "It's always been on her terms."

"This is my mother all over," says Kathy. "At least we're lucky we didn't get the finger."

"*Or the fecking stick*," Loraine adds. "She says she used to get hit around the head with the stick, especially if she didn't want to touch some man's you-know-what with her mouth. She says lots of explicit pictures were taken of her and her sisters, too."

This is sad news to Kathy. Loraine explains how the photos increased when the girls started to develop. As the oldest of the sisters, Mary developed first. She knew what was in store for her younger sisters and tried to protect them by taking on all the abuse herself. But some of the men liked the really young ones, and she couldn't stop her sisters from being forced into the same treatment.

Kathy asks, "Is this what made her so angry at the end of her life?"

"Of course," Loraine tells her. "She says she carried this around with her for too long. And she says she was just about to tell you that before you interrupted, *you rude bitch*."

Kathy finds this hysterical. Clearly, the relationship she had with her mother was a unique one.

Loraine asks if Kathy remembered Maureen, who was eight years old.

Kathy says Maureen only lived a couple of doors away.

Loraine says no, this wasn't in England, this was a Maureen who lived in Ireland, and who was sucked into the paedophile ring as well.

"What about Neela?" Kathy asks.

"*Her, too,*" Loraine insists, "*But what I was just about to tell you when you bloody well interrupted yet again was that Maureen had a sister who was only two, who was never found. They never found her body. Having sex with a two year old would do some damage, wouldn't it? They paid double for that and your grandfather got two pennies that time. He brought in young boys for the men, too.*"

"What about Mary's brother?" Kathy asks. "Was he part of the paedophile ring?"

"*No, he didn't touch us. He didn't have a clue, fecking puff.*" Then Loraine adds, "Someone went off to Australia."

Kathy nods. "My cousin."

"She's going on about someone called Theresa."

"I had a friend named Theresa," Kathy offers.

"No, this was a nun who was in on the ring. She's dead now and Mary's been trying to find her (in the spirit world), but she can't. *Must be rotting in hell,* she says, *the evil bitch. I thought when I died I could find them and hit them but I haven't been able to find them. Not a single one.*"

Kathy says, "That's probably because they're not there, because all those people who abused the children went downstairs."

Loraine says, "*Father O'Leary had twenty-nine of the kids. He preferred the boys, though. Daddy used to bring him some. I never knew how much he got for them, poor mites*."

Kathy asks, "So was my grandfather, my mother's father, the ringleader?"

Loraine says, "You know it."

Kathy nods. "That explains why he took the family out of Ireland."

"He was chased out," Loraine adds.

"I knew he was beat up in the town square," Kathy relates. "He told everyone it was because he refused to join the IRA, but it didn't add up."

"That was just the excuse," Loraine says. "It was because he was one of the paedophile ringleaders. Men came from all over the country for what he offered them. Especially from Cork." Loraine pauses before going on, her voice softer now. "She says: *the angels have come to help me. Four times*."

"Good."

"*But I'm not going to trust them. I never trusted anyone*."

Kathy nods. "That's certainly how she felt."

"Not in life, not in the afterlife. *Even that doctor couldn't save me. The last five years were hard. I went a bit do-lolly. But I still hated everyone. I made out to be worse than I was so I wouldn't have to talk to people and answer their stupid questions.*"

Kathy finds that funny. Then she asks, "When did the abuse stop? At what point in your life did your father stop abusing you?"

"*When he died.*"

"He sexually abused you all his life? All the way up to the end of his life?" Kathy is mortified. "Then he really could have been my father."

"He wasn't." Then Loraine adds, "She's got her arms folded now, and she's gone a bit tame. Now she says she's going to be on her best behaviour."

"She's not fooling me," says Kathy.

"*Aw, feck off.*"

Kathy rolls her eyes. "Just because you can't throw things at me anymore. Well, you can, but you're not going to, are you?"

"*No, I don't want to, really. Can't be bothered. You're not bloody worth* it."

"You know that's not true," Kathy says.

"*Yes, it is true. Now, do you want some cake?*"

Kathy starts laughing. Loraine joins her. Kathy says, "That was her answer to everything. Mum, you know you love me. You loved me, really. You just couldn't show love. That's the problem."

Loraine nods. "*You can't show love if you've never had it. The only time we felt we were being loved was when we were with some bloke who was doing things to us.*"

Kathy adds: "And Susan and I paid the price for it."

Loraine says, "*Sorry.*"

"What?" Kathy gasps. Kathy has heard whispers of abuse before, but never the extent or the details. Despite all that Loraine has conveyed in the reading so far, this is the first time that Kathy seems truly shocked.

"That's right," Loraine tells her. "She says she is sorry."

Kathy has to stop and think about that a while. Then she asks: "What else do you want to get out? What else do you want us to know?"

"*I just want what I've said here to go in the book,*" Loraine tells us. "*I want the truth to come out. I don't trust anyone.*"

Kathy asks, "What will it take to make you be at peace?"

Loraine goes quiet. "*I don't really know. But I'm learning. Guess what? I'm learning to play the piano.*"

"Again?" Kathy asks.

"*And I'm still no good.*"

Finally, a light moment in this reading.

"That is totally my mum," says Kathy. "The laughy-jokey personality that slips in and out between the spite."

"Your mother's funny," Loraine agrees. "You loved her or you hated her, there was no in between. Now she wants to thank you. Not you, Kathy.

Kathy asks, "No?"

"*I want to thank the other one*," Loraine says, looking my way. *The one taking notes*."

"Me?" I ask.

Loraine says, "*Yes, the one that's writing my story. She's all right.*"

I feel my face going pale, horrified. I am here to record Mary's story, not to be a foil for her anger.

"Oh yes," Loraine insists. "She likes you a lot, because you're the one who's going to write up her story."

I have to ask. "Has she been at my house? Watching me?"

"That's right," Loraine says. "She's been there for the last four days."

That would explain my erratic lights.

Kathy asks, "Have you been recently creating mischief at my house, too?"

"*Only twice.*"

"And what was that?" Kathy wants to know.

"*The telly.*"

"That can't be," Kathy insists. "Not my television. It doesn't work."

"*Exactly! And your lights.*"

Kathy nods. "So that was you, again."

"*Always your lights. With the way I mess with them, it's a wonder you can afford your electric bill.*" Then Loraine's voice becomes serious. "She tells me she's feeling better."

Kathy says thoughtfully, "She had a brain disease the last few years of her life, and I haven't heard that breezy banter from her in a very long time."

"She's feeling like she got a lot off her chest," Loraine says. "It was hard because it was her daddy, and you're supposed to love your daddy. And she did. She did try to love him, even though he did all those things to her."

"She idolized him until the day that he died."

"She had to, because he was still her father."

Kathy asks, "Deep down, did you really love Susan and I or did you hate us?"

"*No, I love you dearly and am really proud of you.*"

"So all the things you said and all that talk was just mouthing off?"

"*Definitely. Because as kids, my sisters and I were treated so badly. Like dogs, we had to just do what we were told.*"

"But we did love you," Kathy insists.

"I couldn't accept love. Men told us they loved us, even when they were doing things to us." Loraine is quiet a moment before going on. "She's become very emotional. Now she realizes she was the victim, and made you to feel like victims, too. But she feels like she's finally arriving at a different way of thinking. She's showing me that she's really trying to get better."

"It was so hard to love her," Kathy says. "Because she could be so nasty. I don't know if I can trust her, that she's really changed."

"You can."

Kathy seems torn. "Tell me you're not going to mess up my turkey again at Christmas."

"I won't."

"I'm not sure I believe her. She has thrown things at me," Kathy explains. "Even after she died, things have hit me. Or poked me. Unexplained things. I'm not used to her being kind."

"Isn't that what you wanted?" Loraine asks. *"There's no fecking pleasing you, is there? But you have to admit, I haven't made the windows rattle in a while."*

Kathy says, "But you did make my lights go crazy yesterday."

Loraine scowls. *"Why can't you be more like the one taking the notes, nice and quiet?"*

Kathy shrugs. "She's taking notes and all I did was to be your daughter for all those years." Then Kathy looks at me. "Apparently, Loraine and I are no good at all but you seem to be the golden girl here."

"Right," I say, deadpan. "I'm just fabulous."

We all enjoy a moment of absurd and silly irony.

Then Kathy sighs. "I don't know what to say to her to make her believe that I really loved her."

"She knows," Loraine affirms. "But she's asking where is the music? She says it's getting boring in here again."

Kathy smiles. "That's what I miss. That sharp humour. I do miss her so much."

Loraine says, "She is very remorseful. She tells me she's found a bit of peace now."

"Has she really?"

"She says it's like the burdens are finally coming off of her shoulders."

Kathy asks, "Why did you protect Granddad all those years? Why didn't you say anything sooner or tell anyone about this?"

Loraine says, "*I was embarrassed. But now that it's out, I don't need to talk about it anymore.*"

Kathy asks, "You mean, not until you're ready to bring it up again? To manifest your anger another time?"

"*No. I don't need to dwell on it anymore. Now that it's out, I don't need to hold that anger in any longer. Besides, it's all in the past. Can't change it. I'm done with all that.*"

Kathy asks, "Have you been around me, affecting my moods and making me cantankerous?"

"*Yes.*"

"And are you through with all that now?"

Loraine pauses a moment. Then: "*Maybe.*"

Kathy chuckles.

"*Seriously,*" Loraine continues. "*I am through with that. Time to get on with it. Job done.*"

"You're not just saying that?" Kathy doesn't sound entirely convinced. "What's going to change now?"

"*Me.*"

"And how is that going to happen?"

"*It already has,*" Loraine says. "*Just knowing that you loved me. Because now I believe it.*"

"I did love you," Kathy says. "With all my heart. And Susan, too. You must have known we did. You only had to see us crying after you died to know that. You can't have missed that."

"*I hate tears. I can't stand that.*"

"Is she pleased she's back in Ireland?" Kathy asks.

"*I'm not in Ireland,*" Loraine says. "*I'm here. But yes, I'm glad you had me buried there.*"

"At least we got that right," says Kathy.

"*It's about bloody time!*" This breaks the tension again and we all laugh. Loraine shakes her head. "She really had a wicked sense of humour, didn't she?"

Kathy agrees. "You see? That's the mother I love and remember." Then Kathy asks, "How much more of your story do you need to tell?"

"*That's it. That's all I had to get out.*"

"You're done? You've said everything you wanted to say?"

Loraine says, "She has. She's really calmed down now."

"You mean, until the next time?"

"*No. I really mean it.*"

Kathy asks, "After all the times you've let me down, how can I believe you?"

"*Trust me. Give me the benefit.*"

"Only if you give me the benefit, too."

"*I will,*" says Loraine.

Hope is finally shining in Kathy's eyes. "Are you saying that you finally believe that Susan and I loved you?"

"*Yes, I accept it now,*" says Loraine. "*And I really did love you girls, too. I am dearly proud of you. But...*" she adds with a twinkle in her eye, "*I still prefer the writer*

* * *

After that long reading with Loraine, I went home and listened to the tape again, amazed at the story of a lifetime of abuse that Loraine had revealed. As I had promised, I made a copy of the recording to send to Kathy. Since it was close to Christmas, I took a small Christmas card, added a quick note, and dropped it into the packet before mailing it off.

I didn't see Kathy for another month, but when I did, I asked her about her mother and if she felt that the anger had dissipated.

Kathy reported that she felt that her mother had finally found some peace as Kathy had not experienced any negative or angry activity since the long reading. To verify that her mother had let go of her anger, Kathy had asked her mother to send her a sign. Since robins were Kathy's favourite bird, she had asked her mother's spirit to make a robin speak to her and tell her "hello."

It was an unusual request. I asked Kathy how she expected her mother's spirit to ever be able to pull that off.

"She already has," Kathy replied. "Remember that card that you sent me at Christmas?"

I had almost forgotten about the little card I had dashed off and included in Kathy's mailer with the tape of the session. But then I remembered. It had been a small British Red Cross card, and I had not only signed the inside, but had added a quick note on the front of the card -- an annotation that without knowing anything about Kathy's unusual request, had done the exact thing that Kathy had asked her mother to make happen. And so somehow, Kathy's impossible request to verify that her mother's spirit had finally found some peace had come true after all.

Kathy wanted a special sign. This is the card I had included at the last minute in the packet with the tape of the session.

As Loraine explains, souls can continue to evolve even after death. Following Loraine's own near death experience as chronicled in our previous book, <u>Love and Laughter with Spirit: Meet the Medium Loraine Rees,</u> upon visiting the spirit world, Loraine encountered tormented or guilty souls who were being counselled by special healing energies. The healing spirits sought to help those troubled souls come to terms with their earthly wrongdoings. If they could seek and accept forgiveness, they might finally find peace. The spirit of Kathy's mother was also in need of such peace.

Some people might find it hard to believe that a person's spirit might continue to change and grow after their death. If you question that, consider this: for those of us still on the physical plane, our appreciation of a person and our feelings towards him is not cast in concrete upon his death. The feelings and the emotional relationship we have with a departed person can sometimes change and evolve. We might initially feel anger or bitterness after the death of a loved one. We might even feel that the person has somehow abandoned us, even if he had no control over his death. But after time passes, we might learn to accept the loss and be glad that we were given the gift of that special person in our lives.

If our emotional relationship with a person can change after his death, is it too much to believe that a soul might also continue to evolve? You can't see feelings, but we know our feelings for our loved ones go on even after they've left our world. Might not their feelings go on as well? Just because we can't see them from where we are, does this mean they can't possibly exist?

Fortunately for us, there are people like Loraine who can see and communicate with departed spirits. With Kathy's mother, her spirit needed a chance to get her story out to help dissipate the anger and pain that had been trapped deep inside her for so long. It is only through Loraine's amazing gift and her generosity in giving her time and her talent that this was made possible.

For most people, a reading with Loraine isn't nearly as dramatic. For the vast majority of people who get a special reading, the messages from their loved ones on the other side are overwhelmingly supportive, along with some special details to provide confirmation.

For most of us, that is enough.

I find great comfort in knowing that people like Loraine exist. I feel such people have been given to us to show us that there is more to our souls than the physical world. Just as the world doesn't stop at a sharp edge just because the map maker has run out of paper, it seems to me that the soul doesn't stop because the body has run out of breath. We can shut our eyes and pretend that the world is flat, or we can open our eyes and see that the horizon curves, a curve that will eventually turn into a circle that has no end.

Loraine shows us that there is existence after death. Not only that, but as the experience with Kathy's mother reveals, there is more than life after death; there is a chance for redemption. Given that we all make mistakes, I find that deeply reassuring.

Delving into the unseen can be frightening. While the circumstances of Loraine's brushes with the other side can be scary at times, the end result is a message of hope. Through her immense body of work, with case after case of astonishingly detailed accuracy, Loraine shows us that caring does not end with mortality. Her work shines a light on the journey we will all have to face someday, and promises us all not only eternity but the chance for the greatest gift of all -- love.

ONE FINAL PHOTO

This photo was taken of my son Skyler (center) with two

friends out for an evening in 2016. However, on this digital photo taken on a cell phone, there is another figure – or should I say, parts of another figure – who appears in the photograph. The young woman on the right told us that the mysterious image of a man with a beret and glasses looked like her uncle. However, he had died a week before. Perhaps he appeared in the photo to let her know he was still "with" her.

Enlargement

APPENDIX A – AN INTERVIEW WITH LORAINE

This interview was conducted in the summer of 2011 when we were exploring the idea of creating an archaeology TV series that combined historic research, archaeology, and a medium.

Q: Hi Loraine. Who are you and what do you do?

I'm Loraine Reese. I connect with people's loved ones who have passed on. I also connect to the past, present, and future.

Q: Do you actually see the departed spirits?

I do. I can see them and hear what they're thinking.

Q: Do any other members of your family have this ability?

Yes. I come from Romany gypsy stock. My Great Aunt Jess was a well known medium back in the 1960s. She had lots of books out. She held big séances back in the 1940s and 1950s when it had to be done behind closed doors. It wasn't quite as accepted back then.

Q: You mentioned Romany. Are these gypsies in England?

Yes, now. But they originated in India.

Q: When did you realize you had this ability to connect with the spirit world?

I could always see spirits. I didn't really think much about it until I got to senior school. Then, when I could see things and tell my friends what was going to happen, it made quite an impact, although it wasn't always good. One time I told my friend that her mum had just died. I wasn't very tactful, I just said it. She didn't believe me and was quite upset, insisting I was wrong. After that we didn't see her for a few weeks because her mother had died.

Q: How do people benefit from your gift?

When they lose people tragically or even if they lose their loved one to a natural cause, to know I can bring them information that only the deceased would know gives them peace of mind that life goes on.

Q: How do you get your information?

It is given to me through Ramos, my main spirit guide. He was an Egyptian. Ramos brings people's loved ones through to me.

Q: How long has he been giving you information?

As long as I can remember, although I didn't know where it was coming from until I was a teenager.

Q: Is he giving you information right now?

Yes, he is. He gets especially interested when I'm talking about him.

Q: He likes the attention?

He loves it.

Q: We were thinking of doing an archaeology show that had a psychic. Is this something you would be interested in?

Yes, definitely. Obviously I don't know a lot about history because that's not my field. What I do is to link in with spirits who have crossed over. For the purpose of this type of project, the less I know about history, the better.

Q: Can you tell us a little about Ramos?

He was an Egyptian man, born before Christ. He was connected with Pharaoh Ramses III and was his right hand man. At least that what I always believed. Interestingly enough, I went to Cairo to see for myself if Pharaoh Ramses III had a connection with someone named Ramos. When I arrived in Cairo I went to the Egyptology museum but the exhibition on Ramses III was closed. I was disappointed, of course, but as we took the tour bus to the next town, we picked up a man who turned out to be an Egyptology professor at the local institute and an expert on Pharaoh Ramses III. I asked him to tell me about the reign of Ramses III. Without explaining to him why I wanted to know, he said, "Well, the most important person in his council was a man named Ramos." That was exciting to have independent confirmation since I hadn't even mentioned Ramos. The historian went on to tell me about Ramos' role in the royal court. Apparently, Ramos had 27 wives.

Q: Wow. What was his life like at the Egyptian royal court?

He was the main person who dealt with law. He was such a trusted advisor of the pharaoh that when Ramses III died, Ramos died with him.

Q: They killed him?

Not exactly. After Pharaoh Ramses III died, as they were enclosing the tomb, they sent Ramos down into the tomb chambers to guard the body. Then they closed him in. He had to sit there and guard the body as they closed the tomb and he perished.

Q: What kind of religious and spiritual aspects did they believe in at that time?

The worshiped the moon, the stars, and the planets. They were very much into the zodiac. They also believed in aliens. I don't know if you've seen a lot of images on the Egyptian walls but they drew a lot of alien encounters where the aliens came down in a ray of light. They called them "the light beings." It is very interesting that around the same time, the Aztecs were going through the same thing and drawing similar pictures. From different parts of the earth, they were having the same experiences. They both worshiped these "light beings."

Q: What was the political climate like when Ramos was helping Ramses III?

He was always fearful for his life. There were always invasions going on in the world and at that time, anything could happen. But at the same time, Ramses III was a peaceful king. It was a relatively peaceful reign and a lot of Ramos' time was spent assisting Ramses and assisting with the women.

Q: Women?

Ramos did like the ladies. In fact, he quite likes the blonde lady over there [producer Donna Love who directed and filmed the interview]. **He's quite a flirt, our Ramos.**

Q: Did he have children?

He fathered at least 30 children. Some died very young.

Q: Was Ramses III a good leader?

He was. He was given the title because of inheritance. He didn't want to be the pharaoh or the leader and didn't go after power. That is why his reign was so peaceful.

Q: Did he care about his people?

He did.

Q: What was Ramses III like? Did he have a family?

He had a wife and children. Actually, I've just been told he had five wives, but not all at once.

Q: Was he the son of Ramses II?

Yes, who was the son of Ramses I. There is not a lot written about Ramses III. He was the start of what Egyptologists call the New Generation.

Q: People are interested in where we come from and trying to re-discover what has been lost. Could you or Ramos give us insights on historical sites?
Definitely. I can give you an example. When I was in Rome at the Coliseum, something unusual happened to me. It was like a black and white movie was playing in front of my eyes. I could see women shouting and children crying. It was very violent.

Q: Was this a scene from the past?

Yes. It was a very unusual experience. As the tour guide was talking, I continued to "see" these images, like movie clips, and I could tell when the guide was correct or not from the images I was seeing. It was exactly like watching a black and white movie from the past, but I was fully awake. I must have looked odd with my attention focused on something no one else could see because a few people in the group asked me if I was all right.

Q: Do you think Ramos would like to visit with you some of the places where he lived during his life?

Definitely. He wasn't actually in Cairo. He was based down in the Valley of the Kings.

Q: Sometimes dig sites include human remains. Would you think you would be able to glean insights from examining things like that?

Certainly. I do psychometry where I hold a piece of jewellery or some object and I can get an insight into the life of the person who owned it.

Q: You can get that kind of information just by just touching an object someone owned?

Yes, I can see their life, what was important to them, and usually how they passed.

Q: Do you actually "see" them and what they looked like?

I do.

Q: What if there were bones in the site?

I've never held a human bone before, but obviously, you can't get an object more personal than that.

Q: We feel that archaeology is a good way to connect with our past and discover things that have been lost in our human heritage. Would working with a medium like you and your spirit guide help us build a deeper understanding?

I feel it would because I would be dealing with people's energy and how they felt within their environment. Also it would give a good insight on their spiritual beliefs. At the moment, we live in a very materialistic world. Back then, it could have been very different.

Q: Would you be able to bring us into their world?

Yes, into their environment and their feelings. And obviously their sense of being and their purpose.

Q: Would you be interested in this type of project?

Definitely. I think it would be very interesting.

Q: What does Ramos think about it?

He would be quite excited about it, especially if there were going to be lots of blondies involved.

APPENDIX B: WHAT PEOPLE SAY
ABOUT LORAINE.
From her *"Loraine Rees Clairvoyant Medium"* Facebook Page

OMG - Loraine Rees Medium Clairvoyant was just phenomenal as always -- Everyone went away just gob smacked, enlightened and happy. Thank you so much. See you in 6 months.

Thank you for my reading last night, amazing...... all the names coming back to me now! Please let us know when you are in the area again, we have more people interested in seeing you. Hope the journey back wasn't too bad.

Amazing reading tonight - still buzzing from all the information and more and more things are falling into place. Thank you and Good Luck in Las Vegas.

Had such a good reading with u tonight! Thank u, we were all very happy! :) have a great time in Vegas!

Hi Loraine. Thank you for the reading today. Made me feel a lot better about myself and every thing you told me was true. Just waiting to see if a man does come into my life.

Loraine's 13th May show at Leverington will raise money for my daughter Millie. She was born disabled as my placenta had started to come away and her brain was starved from oxygen so I had a emergency section. The first couple off days was touch and go if she would survive or not. She was in intensive care for nearly 3 weeks before they would let her home with me. She has to go back every 3 months for check ups. She's doing really well, the money I get will be going towards getting her some sensory lights for her bedroom as we had some on loan. She loved them :) please come along :)

Great show last night Loraine, very fun! Sadly me and my auntie were not picked out maybe next time ;)

Had a reading today with Lorraine. Firstly, she's a lovely friendly lady who makes you feel at ease straight away. The reading itself was mind blowing. The things she picked up on were spot-on. I will definitely be booking again.

Totally blown away by my reading yesterday - you are amazing. Thank you so much.

Just wanted to thank you although words are not enough, but also to share with the world what a special lady you are. I came to see you Feb. 2011 after losing my baby girl whom you assured me was ok as she came thru during the reading. You gave me hope that I would have a baby as you told me I would have a baby early in 2012 and would be a girl. I'm sat here holding my BABY GIRL who was born on Tues 7th Feb. Thank you from the bottom of my heart.

I went to see [popular medium] S___ M ____tonight and she wasn't a patch on you.

APPENDIX C: BOOKS BY DR. GARY SCHWARTZ

Gary Schwartz, PhD is one of the leading researchers in the field of parapsychology who explores psychic phenomena and related topics using scientific principles and techniques. He received his PhD in psychology from Harvard University in 1971 and was assistant professor at Harvard for five years before serving as professor of psychology and psychiatry at Yale University. Currently he is Professor of Psychology, Medicine, Neurology, Psychiatry, and Surgery at the University of Arizona as well as Director of the Laboratory for Advances in Consciousness and Health. Here is a selected bibliography of some of his works.

Gary E. Schwartz and John Edward (Foreword), "The Sacred Promise: How Science is Discovering Spirit's Collaboration with us in our Daily Lives," 2011, Atria Books/Beyond Words. ISBN 978-1-58270-258-2

Gary E. Schwartz, William L. Simon, and Richard Cormona (Foreword), "The Energy Healing Experiments: Science Reveals our Natural Power to Heal, 2007, Atria books. ISBN 978-0-7432-9239-9

Gary E. Schwartz and William L. Simon, "The G.O.D. Experiments; How Science is Discovering God in Everything, Including Us, 2006, Atria Books. ISBN 978-0-7434-7740-6

Gary E. Schwartz and William L. Simon, "The Truth About Medium: Extraordinary Experiments with the real Allison DuBois of NBC's Medium and other Remarkable Psychics, 2005, Hampton Roads Publishing Company. ISBN 1-57174-459-2

Gary E. Schwartz, William L. Simon, and Deepak Chopra (Foreword). The Afterlife Experiments, 2002, Simon and Schuster International. ISBN 978-0-7434-3659-5

Gary E. Schwartz, PhD and Linda G. S. Russek, Living Energy Universe: A Fundamental Discovery that Transforms Science and Medicine, 1999, Hampton Roads Publishing Co. ISBN 978-1-5717-4170-7

Richard J. Davidson (Editor), Gary E. Schwartz (Editor), David Shapiro, Consciousness and Self-Regulation, Advances in Research and Theory Volume 4, 1986, Plenum Press. ISBN 0-306-42048-1

GLOSSARY OF PARAPSYCHOLOGY TERMS

Selected terms and definitions extracted from the online Glossary of
Parapsychology by Michael Daniels, PhD, reprinted with permission.
For the complete glossary, see: www.psychicscience.org/paraglos.aspx

Animal Psi
> Paranormal abilities exhibited by animals. Also known as
> "Anpsi".

Apport/Deport
> An apport is a physical object which appears in a way that
> cannot be explained (seeming to come from nowhere). Often
> associated with the séance room and physical mediumship. Also
> called materialization or teleportation. A deport is a physical
> object which seems to disappear.

Automatic Writing
> The ability to write intelligible messages without conscious
> control or knowledge of what is being written. Also called
> automatism or dissociation.

Ba
> Also called Ka. Ancient Egyptian concept of a person's essence
> or soul, believed to be immortal.

Cipher Test
> A coded message left by a person who intends to communicate
> the cipher after death.

Clairaudience
> The paranormal obtaining of information by hearing sounds or
> voices. See also clairvoyance, clairsentience.

Clairsentience
> A somewhat archaic term that refers to the paranormal obtaining
> of information using faculties other than vision or hearing, such
> as feeling.

Clairvoyance
> A term that initially referred to the paranormal obtaining of
> information visually, through imagery. In modern usage it can

also be used more generally to encompass all information obtained paranormally.

Cold Reading/Hot Reading

A cold reading is given with no prior knowledge of the sitter. Often a mixture of very general statements which could apply to anyone, together with inferences made from cues presented by the sitter (e.g., physical appearance, clothes, tone of voice, statements made). A hot reading is one given in which prior knowledge of the sitter has been obtained, often using devious or fraudulent means.

Collective Apparition

An apparition seen simultaneously by more than one person.

Confederate

A person who secretly provides information to a fraudulent psychic or mentalist.

Cosmic Consciousness

A blissful experience in which the person becomes aware of the whole universe as a living being. See also altered state of consciousness, mystical experience.

Crisis Apparition

An apparition in which a person is seen within a few hours of an important crisis such as death, accident or sudden illness.

Déjà Vu

A person's feeling that current events have been experienced before.

Direct Voice/Indirect Voice

Direct voice is one heard in a séance which does not seem to emanate from any person. The voice may seem to come out of thin air, or from a trumpet used specifically for this purpose. Indirect Voice is when an entity appears to speak using the vocal apparatus of the medium. Often the voice will sound different from the medium's.

Discarnate Entity

A spirit, soul, or non-material entity. Often used to refer to the personality of a deceased individual.

Double Blind

An experimental procedure in which neither the subject nor experimenter is aware of key features of the experiment.

Dowsing

The paranormal detection of underground water or mineral deposits (or lost persons and objects) using a divining rod (either a forked rod or sometimes a pair of L-shaped rods) or pendulum.

Drop-in Communicator

An uninvited communicator or energy who 'drops in' at a sitting.

Extrasensory Perception (ESP)

Paranormal acquisition of information. Includes clairvoyance, telepathy and precognition. See also psi.

False Awakening

An experience in which a person believes he or she has woken up, but actually is still dreaming.

Glossolalia

Unintelligible speech generally uttered in a dissociated or trance state. Also known as "speaking in tongues". Also called xenoglossy.

Guide

A spirit who is believed to assist a person's spiritual journey. Also called a spirit guide or guardian angel.

Healing

Generally indicates cures that cannot be explained in terms of accepted medical principles. Also called faith healing, psychic healing, spirit cures. This may involve the laying of hands. In absent healing, the healer is not in physical contact with the patient. Another specific type is psychic surgery which is actual or simulated surgery carried out by healers.

Hypnagogic/Hypnopompic Imagery

Hypnagogic imagery occurs in the hypnagogic state (while dropping off to sleep). Hynpopompic imagery occurs in the hypnopompic state (while waking up).

Kirlian Photography

A photographic method involving high frequency electric current, discovered by S.D. & V. Kirlian in the Soviet Union. Kirlian photographs often show coloured halos, luminous phenomena, or "auras" surrounding objects. Also called spirit photography or thoughtography.

Medium

A person believed to act as an intermediary between discarnate entities and the living.

Near-Death Experience (NDE)

Experiences of people after they have been pronounced clinically dead, or been very close to death. Typical features of the NDE are an OBE, life review, a tunnel experience, light, coming to a boundary (marking death), seeing dead friends and relatives, experiencing a loving or divine presence and being told to return. Occasionally NDEs can be frightening and distressing. NDEs often have profound effects on the person's later life. Also called cerebral anoxia.

Null hypothesis

The hypothesis that experimental results are due to chance.

Out of Body Experience (OBE, OOBE)

A fully conscious experience in which the person's centre of awareness appears to be outside of the physical body. Can be related to autoscopy or the near-death experience.

Palmistry

The art of assessing a person's character and forecasting life events by examining features of the hand.

Paranormal Dreams

Dreams in which the dream imagery provides paranormal knowledge (e.g., ESP or precognition) or a paranormal experience. Specific types of paranormal dreams include announcing dreams (believed to announce an individual's rebirth via reincarnation), lucid dreams (in which the dreamer can control what happens in the dream giving a feeling of great freedom), simultaneous dreams where elements correspond closely with those in the dream of another person and veridical dreams which correspond to real events (past, present or future) that are unknown to the dreamer.

Parapsychology

Term coined by J.B. Rhine to refer to the experimental and quantitative study of paranormal or supernatural phenomena. Now generally used instead of "psychical research" to refer to all scientific investigation of the paranormal.

Percipient

Person who receives impressions in an ESP test. See also agent, subject.

Poltergeist

German word meaning "noisy or troublesome spirit". Poltergeist activity may include unexplained noises, movements of objects, outbreaks of fire, floods, pricks or scratches to a person's body. Unlike hauntings, which are associated with specific locations, poltergeists typically focus on a person (the focal person or poltergeist agent) who is often a young child or adolescent. Many physical mediums experienced poltergeist activity in their childhood.

Precognition

The paranormal awareness of future events. Also called prediction, premonition, prophecy.

Psi

A term used to encompass all paranormal abilities. Includes both ESP and PK abilities.

Psychic

A person who exhibits psi ability (also used as an adjective).

Psychokinesis (PK)

The paranormal influence of the mind on physical events and processes.

Psychometry

Obtaining paranormal knowledge using a physical object as a focus. Also known as object reading.

Radiesthesia

Theories based on the assumption that living organisms emit some kind of radiation or emanation that is capable of being detected using instruments or by dowsing. Associated with aura and radionics.

Raudive Voices

Intelligible voices recorded on magnetic tape under conditions of silence or white noise which are heard only when the tape is played. A phenomenon discovered by Konstantin Raudive. Also called instrumental transcommunication or pareidolia.

Regression

(a) a statistical technique that enables predictions to be made from a set of data.
(b) a technique used in hypnosis, involving suggesting to hypnotized persons that they are returning to an earlier time.

Sometimes the regression occurs spontaneously, without suggestion. Includes past-life regression.

Reincarnation

The belief that some aspect of a person's being (e.g., consciousness, personality, or soul) survives death and can be reborn in a new body at some future date. Reincarnation is often seen as a repeating cycle of death and rebirth in which future lives are influenced by past and present actions through the law of karma ("you shall reap what you sow").

Remote Viewing (RV)

An ESP procedure in which a percipient attempts to become aware psychically of the experience of an agent who is at a distant, unknown target location.

Sheep-Goat Effect

Effect, discovered by the parapsychologist Gertrude Schmeidler, in which "sheep" (people who believe in the psi effect) score higher than mean chance expectation (MCE) on psi tests, while "goats" (people who do not believe in the psi effect) score lower than MCE.

Significance

Results of an experiment are said to be statistically significant when they are very unlikely to be due to chance (and hence, in a psi test, are more likely to be due to psi). The chance probability is reported as the "significance level". To be considered significant, the chance probability must generally be less than 1 in 20 (5%, or 0.05).

Tarot

A special deck of cards (usually 78) used in fortune telling.

Telekinesis

Paranormal movement of objects.

Telepathy

Paranormal awareness of another person's experience (thoughts, feelings, etc.). In practice it is difficult to distinguish between telepathy and clairvoyance. See also ESP.

Trance

A dissociated state of consciousness, generally involving reduced awareness of surroundings and external events.

ABOUT THE AUTHOR

Mary Ross spent 10 years as a scientist, mapping unexplored rock formations of Alaska and teaching college classes on the side. She moved to England in 2001 and began her doctoral research in adult education, exploring ways of combining right brain with left brain modes of thinking to maximize a student's academic potential.

After a chance meeting with Loraine Rees in 2007, Loraine predicted that Mary would be the one to document Loraine's work. Over the next four years, Mary investigated Loraine's practice which resulted in her first book on the subject, <u>Love and Laughter with Spirit: Meet the Medium Loraine Rees</u>, published in 2011.

<u>Troubled Spirits with Medium Loraine Rees</u>, Mary's second book on the medium, continues to record Loraine's work including mystifying ghost walks and the development of the author's own abilities to supplement Loraine's readings through drawings. Mary feels she was chosen to document Loraine's work because both she and Loraine have "been there," having each experienced clinical death conditions but were resuscitated and brought back to life.

Their third collaboration, <u>Deep Inside the Mind: Releasing Your Inner Light,</u> directly channels wisdom from the other side for modern audiences to find their own connections to the spirit world.

Made in United States
North Haven, CT
15 September 2024

56918272R00114